THE PLAY OF
THE DIARY OF
ANNE FRANK

Frances Goodrich and Albert Hackett

Introduction by Ray Speakman

Notes and questions by Alison Jenkins
and Ray Speakman

Series Editor: Lawrence Till

Heinemann Educational Publishers
Halley Court, Jordan Hill, Oxford OX2 8EJ
a division of Reed Educational & Professional Publishing Ltd
MELBOURNE   AUCKLAND   FLORENCE   PRAGUE   MADRID   ATHENS
SINGAPORE   TOKYO   SAO PAULO   PORTSMOUTH NH   MEXICO CITY
IBADAN   GABORONE   JOHANNESBURG   KAMPALA   NAIROBI

First published in the *Hereford Plays* series by Heinemann Educational 1991
First published in the *Heinemann Plays* series 1995

98 99 00 01 02 12 11 10 9 8 7 6 5 4

A catalogue record for this book is available from the British Library on request.

ISBN 0 435 233149

Cover design by Keith Pointing
Original design by Jeffrey White Creative Associates; adapted by Jim Turner.
Typeset by CentraCet Limited, Cambridge
Printed by Clays Ltd, St Ives plc

CONTENTS

PREFACE

In this edition of the play of *The Diary of Anne Frank*, you will find notes, questions and activities to help in studying the play in class, particularly at GCSE level.

The introduction provides background information on Anne Frank and her family, the historical context in which they lived and the particular circumstances which gave rise to the writing of Anne's diary.

The activities at the end of the book range from straightforward *Keeping Track* questions which can be tackled at the end of each act to focus close attention on what is happening in the play, to more detailed work on character, drama and further activities in the *Explorations* section.

There is also a bibliography detailing other books of related interest.

If you are already using the Floodlight edition of the play of *The Diary of Anne Frank*, you will find that the page numbering in the actual playscript is the same allowing the two editions to be easily used side by side.

INTRODUCTION

The Diary of Anne Frank

This play is based upon the diary kept by Anne Frank while she and her family were in hiding from the Nazis in Holland during the Second World War.

The Rise of Hitler and the Nazis

Immediately after the First World War and again in the late twenties and early thirties Germany suffered severe economic problems which led to high inflation and unemployment. There was also a sense of national humiliation at the way the country had been treated under the Treaty of Versailles which ended the war in 1919. Throughout this period the National Socialist German Workers party (the Nazi party) steadily recruited more supporters. The party's leader, Adolf Hitler, blamed the country's economic troubles not only on the weaknesses of the government, but also upon the Jews. He made the Jews a scapegoat for everything that was wrong with Germany – just as some people today blame specific groups for what they believe is wrong in their own country. In the elections of 1933 Hitler and his party gained power in the German parliament, and shortly afterwards he seized absolute power; he became a dictator.

Hitler's Treatment of the Jews and the 'Final Solution'

Almost immediately Hitler introduced a boycott of Jewish shopkeepers, doctors and lawyers. Jewish civil servants were then dismissed from their posts and in 1935 the Nuremberg Laws deprived Jews of German citizenship and banned marriage between Germans and Jews. By 1938 German Jews had no protection under the law. On the night of November 9th, 1938, Jewish property all over Germany was smashed by the SA ('Stormtroopers') and SS ('Protection Squad'). It was clear that Hitler wanted the whole of the Jewish population removed from Germany. Emigration was suggested by some, including a scheme to resettle all German Jews in Madagascar, but he rejected this. So obsessed was Hitler by his anti-Jewish feelings that in 1941 he began the programme of extermination known as the 'Final Solution'. His first step was the Decree of Identification which insisted that all Jews wear a yellow Star of David – which the characters in the play talk about in the first scene. This Decree was followed by mass deportations of Jews to concentration camps at Chelmo, Auschwitz, Belzec, Sobibor, and Treblinka. These camps, all in Poland, began putting Jews to death in gas chambers in 1942. More camps followed: Bergen-Belsen, Buchenwald and Dachau, for instance. By the time the camps were liberated it is estimated that six million Jews had died in Europe as a result of Hitler's 'Final Solution'.

The Story of Anne Frank

Anne Frank's family had lived in Frankfurt, Germany, for many generations. Her father, Otto Frank, was born in 1889 and grew up as part of a prosperous banker's family. During the First World War (1914–18) he and his two brothers served in the German army. After the war Otto worked in the family bank and it was at this time that he met Edith Hollander, the daughter of a factory owner. She was eleven years younger than Otto. They married in 1925 and had two daughters, Margot, born in 1926, and Annelies Marie (Anne), born on June 12th, 1929.

In 1933 when Otto Frank saw the beginnings of the anti-Jewish boycott, he decided to take his family to live in Amsterdam, Holland, where there was a long tradition of religious tolerance. The family lived in a house on Merwedeplein, a pleasant and prosperous district in the southern part of the city, and Anne and Margot went to a Montessori school nearby. The family and Otto's business settled into a happy and prosperous way of life. However, when the Germans invaded Holland in May 1940, bringing with them their numerous anti-Jewish laws, Otto decided to take his family into hiding – known at the time as 'diving'.

With the help of his Dutch staff, Mr Kraler, Mr Koophuis, Miep Gies and Elli Vossen, Otto prepared a hiding place for his family and for the family of Mr Van Daan who worked in Otto's company. On July 5th, 1942, Margot received a letter instructing her to report to a 'labour camp' – which, in effect, meant a concentration camp. As a result Otto hurried his plans along and on July 6th the family moved into the 'Secret Annex'. The hiding place was on the two upper floors of his workplace. There were in fact two houses making up the company premises – one facing the street, and one immediately behind it. 'The House in Back' was used by the two families and Anne intended to use this name as the title of the story she hoped would be published after the war. At first there were seven people crammed into the 'Secret Annex', the Franks and their two daughters, and the Van Daans and their son, Peter. Later they were joined by an acquaintance, Albert Dussel.

'Diving' – going into hiding – was made possible by the bravery of the four people who were willing to risk their lives by keeping those hiding supplied with food. Anne wrote in her diary:

There are a great number of organisations, such as 'The Free Netherlands' which forge identity cards, find hiding places for people, and work for young men in hiding, and it is amazing how much noble, unselfish work these people are doing risking their own lives to help and save others.

The eight people in hiding had to cease to exist as far as the outside world was concerned. As the play describes, they had to take great care not to be seen or heard. Anne read and studied to keep herself busy, and keeping her diary became an important pastime. She treated her diary as her closest friend and called it 'Kitty'.

News from the outside world came from friends and from the radio:

> I get frightened when I think of close friends who have now been delivered into the hands of the cruellest brutes that walk the earth. All because they are Jews. Every now and then, when Miep lets out something about what has happened to a friend, Mummy and Mrs Van Daan always begin to cry, so Miep thinks it better not to tell us any more.

In spite of the dreadful things going on around them, Anne always remained hopeful:

> Believe me, if you had been shut up for a year and a half, it can get too much for you some days. In spite of all justice and thankfulness, you can't crush your feelings. Cycling, dancing, whistling, looking out into the world, feeling you, to know that I am free – that's what I long for; still I mustn't show it, because I sometimes think if all eight of us began to pity ourselves, or went about with discontented faces, where would it lead us?

As the play shows, Anne did not find it easy to live with the others in hiding. She loved her sister, Margot, but became annoyed with the constant comparisons Mrs Frank made between the two girls. Her mother irritated Anne most of the time; she quarrelled frequently with Mr Dussel and found Mrs Van Daan 'silly'. Although she adored her father, she felt awkward about confiding everything to him, so her diary became very important to her. In the early days Anne found Peter Van Daan 'immature' but as time went on she was drawn closer and closer to him.

The family stayed in hiding for two years, until 4th August, 1944. Although the play suggests the circumstances of their discovery, it is not in fact known how their hiding place was betrayed. They were taken to a camp in Holland and from there to Auschwitz. The Gestapo later moved Anne and Margot from Auschwitz to Bergen-Belsen where, in early 1945, they died of typhus. The Van Daans, Mrs Frank and Mrs Dussel all died in Auschwitz. Only Otto Frank survived.

After the war Otto returned to Amsterdam. Here he discovered that Mr Kraler and Mr Koophuis had been imprisoned for helping the Frank family. Miep and Elli had escaped arrest, and it was Miep who had found and kept Anne's diary. At first Otto wanted to burn everything which remained of the time in the attic, but his friends persuaded him to publish the diary. In 1947 Anne's diary appeared under the title, 'Het Achterhuis' ('The Annex'). Since then more than eighteen million copies have been sold. In 1953 Otto married Elfriede Markovits, also a survivor of Auschwitz. They lived in Switzerland where in 1980, aged ninety one, Otto died.

Anne's story is a fragment of what has come to be known as the Holocaust. The Nazis took the lives of almost six million 'normal human beings . . . because they were Jews; because they were the children of their parents; because evil men triumphed over sanity and civilised human feelings'

(Martin Gilbert). The horrors of what happened in Germany between 1933 and 1945, the torment suffered by so many individuals, is a story not only of anti-Semitism but of racism. Nor is it only about the past, or even Europe; it is about now and many other areas of the world where racism follows its twisted logic towards a 'final solution'.

Outside Jerusalem there is a monument known as 'Yad Vashem' – which means 'a Place and a Name':

> Even unto them will I give
> in mine house and within my walls
> a Place and a Name
> better than of sons and of daughters,
> I will give them an everlasting name;
> that shall not be cut off.
>
> *(Book of Isaiah)*

This is what Anne's story does, gives an 'everlasting name' to what happened in Europe earlier this century and ensures that we resist being 'cut off' from the horrors of racism wherever it occurs.

The Diary of Anne Frank

List of Characters

The Diary of Anne Frank was produced at the Phoenix Theatre, London, on the 29th November 1956, with the following cast of characters:

(in the order of their appearance)

MR FRANK	George Voskovec
MIEP GIES	Jane Jordan Rogers
MRS VAN DAAN	Miriam Karlin
MR VAN DAAN	Max Bacon
PETER VAN DAAN	Harry Lockart
MRS FRANK	Vera Fusek
MARGOT FRANK	Clarissa Stolz
ANNE FRANK	Perlita Neilson
MR KRALER	Kynaston Reeves
MR DUSSEL	John Gabriel

Directed by FRITH BANBURY
Setting by BORIS ARONSON

Amen, Oh-mein
Amsterdam, Ahm'-ster-dahm
Anne, Ah'-nah or the familiar Ah'-nee
Anneke, Ah'nah'kah
Anneline, Ah-nah-lynn
Auschwitz, Aow'-schvitz
Belsen, Bell'-sen
Buchenwald, Buch'-en-vald
Delphi, Dell'-fie
Dirk, Dee'-urk
Dussel, Duss'-ell
Edith, Ae'-dith
Frank, Frahnk
Hallensteins, Ha'-len-stains
Hilversum, Hill'-ver-sum
Jan, Yan
Jopie, Yo'-pee

Kerli, Care'lee
Kraler, Krah'-ler
liefje, Leaf'yah
Margot, Mar'gott
Mauthausen, Maut'-how-sen
Mazeltov, Mah'-zel-tahv
Miep, Meep
Mouschi, Moo'-shee
Otto, Ah'-toe
Peter, Pay'-ter
Petronella, Pet-row-nell'-ah
Putti, Poo'-tee
Rotterdam, Rah'-ter-dahm
Van Daan, Fahn Dahn
Wessels, Vess'-ells
Westertoren, Vess'ter-tor-en
Wilhelmina, Vil-hel-mee'-nah

THE DIARY OF ANNE FRANK*

ACT ONE

Scene One

The top floors of a warehouse in Amsterdam, Holland. November 1945. Late afternoon.

MR FRANK enters. He is weak and ill and is making a supreme effort at self-control. His clothes are threadbare. He carries a small rucksack. A scarf catches his eye. He takes it down, puts it around his neck, then wanders towards the couch, but stops as he sees the glove. He picks it up. Suddenly all control is gone. He breaks down and weeps. MIEP GIES enters up the stairs. She is a Dutch girl of about twenty-two, pregnant now. She is compassionate and protective in her attitude towards MR FRANK. She has been a stenographer and secretary in his business. She has her coat and hat on, ready to go home. A small silver cross hangs at her throat.

MIEP   Are you all right, Mr Frank?

MR FRANK   (*quickly controlling himself*) Yes, Miep, yes.

MIEP   Everyone in the office has gone home – it's after six. Don't stay up here, Mr Frank. What's the use of torturing yourself like this?

---

* NB. Paragraph 3 on page ii of this Edition regarding photocopying and video-recording should be carefully read.

MR FRANK   I've come to say good-bye – I'm leaving here, Miep.

MIEP   What do you mean? Where are you going? Where?

MR FRANK   I don't know yet. I haven't decided.

MIEP   Mr Frank, you can't leave here. This is your home.
Amsterdam is your home. Your business is here,
waiting for you. You're needed here. Now that the war
is over, there are things that . . .

MR FRANK   I can't stay in Amsterdam, Miep. It has too many
memories for me. Everywhere there's something – the
house we lived in – the school – the street organ
playing out there. I'm not the person you used to
know, Miep. I'm a bitter old man. Forgive me. I
shouldn't speak to you like this – after all that you did
for us – the suffering . . .

MIEP   No. No. It wasn't suffering. You can't say we suffered.

MR FRANK   I know what you went through, you and Mr Kraler. I'll
remember it as long as I live. Come, Miep. (*He
remembers his rucksack, crosses below the table to the
couch and picks up his rucksack.*)

MIEP   Mr Frank, did you see? There are some of your papers
here. (*She takes a bundle of papers from the shelves,
then crosses below the table to* MR FRANK.) We found
them in a heap of rubbish on the floor after – after you
left.

MR FRANK   Burn them. (*He opens his rucksack and puts the glove
in it.*)

MIEP   But, Mr Frank, there are letters, notes . . .

MR FRANK   Burn them. All of them.

MIEP   Burn this? (*She hands him a worn, velour-covered book.*)

MR FRANK   (*quietly*) Anne's diary. (*He opens the diary and reads.*) 'Monday, the sixth of July, nineteen hundred and forty-two.' (*To* MIEP.) Nineteen hundred and forty-two. Is it possible, Miep? Only three years ago. (*He reads.*) 'Dear Diary, since you and I are going to be great friends, I will start by telling you about myself. My name is Anne Frank. I am thirteen years old. I was born in Germany the twelfth of June, nineteen twenty-nine. As my family is Jewish, we emigrated to Holland when Hilter came to power.'

MR FRANK   } (*together*)   'My father started a business, importing
ANNE'S VOICE }   spice and herbs. Things went well for us until nineteen forty. Then the War came and the Dutch – (*He turns the page.*) defeat, followed by the arrival of the Germans. Then things got very bad for the Jews.'

(MR FRANK'S *voice dies out as* ANNE'S VOICE *grows stronger.*)

ANNE   You could not do this and you could not do that. They forced father out of his business. We had to wear yellow stars. I had to turn in my bike. I couldn't go to a Dutch school any more. I couldn't go to the cinema, or ride in an automobile, or even on a streetcar, and a million other things. But somehow we children still managed to have fun. Yesterday, father told me we were going into hiding. Where, he wouldn't say. At five o'clock this morning mother woke me and told me to hurry and get dressed. I was to put on as many clothes as I could. It would look too suspicious if we walked along carrying suitcases. It wasn't until we were on our way that I learned where we were going. Our hiding place was to be upstairs in the building where father used to have his business. Three other people were coming in with us – the Van Daans and their son Peter. Father knew the Van Daans but we had never met them.

(*The sound of distant ships' sirens is heard.*)

Scene Two

Early morning. July 1942.

The three members of the VAN DAAN *family are waiting for the* FRANKS *to arrive.* MR VAN DAAN *is smoking a cigarette and watching his wife with a nervous eye. His overcoat and suit are expensive and well-cut.* MRS VAN DAAN *is sitting on the couch. She is a pretty woman in her early forties and is clutching her possessions: a hat-box, a handbag and an attractive straw carry-all.* PETER VAN DAAN *is standing at the window in the room. He is a shy, awkward boy of sixteen. He wears a cap, a short overcoat, and long Dutch trousers, like 'plus fours'. All the* VAN DAANS *have the conspicuous yellow Star of David on the left breast of their clothing.*

MRS V. DAAN   Something's happened to them. I know it.

MR V. DAAN   Now, Kerli!

MRS V. DAAN Mr Frank said they'd be here at seven o'clock. He
said . . .

MR V. DAAN They have two miles to walk. You can't expect . . .

MRS V. DAAN They've been picked up.

(*The door below opens.*)

That's what happened. They've been taken.

(MR VAN DAAN *indicates that he hears someone
coming.*)

MR V. DAAN You see?

(MR FRANK *comes up the stairwell from below.*)

MR FRANK Mrs Van Daan, Mr Van Daan. (*He shakes hands with
them. He moves to* PETER *and shakes his hand.*) There
were too many of the Green Police on the streets – we
had to take the long way round.

(MIEP, *not pregnant now,* MARGOT, MR KRALER, *and* MRS
FRANK *come up the stairs.* MARGOT *is eighteen,
beautiful, quiet and shy. She carries a leatherette
hold-all and a large brown paper bag, which she puts
on the table.* KRALER *is a Dutchman, dependable and
kindly. He wears a hearing aid in his ear and carries
two brief-cases.* MRS FRANK *is a young mother, gently
bred and reserved. She, like* MR FRANK, *has a slight
German accent. She carries a leatherette shopping bag
and her handbag. We see the Star of David
conspicuous on the* FRANKS' *clothing.* KRALER
acknowledges the VAN DAANS, *moves to the shelves and
checks their contents.* MIEP *empties her straw bag of
the clothes it contains and piles them on the table.*)

MRS FRANK   Anne?

(ANNE FRANK *comes quickly up the stairs. She is thirteen, quick in her movements, interested in everything and mercurial in her emotions. She wears a cape, long wool socks and carries a school bag.*)

MR FRANK   My wife, Edith. Mr and Mrs Van Daan.

(MRS FRANK *shakes* MR VAN DAAN'S *hand, then hurries across to shake hands with* MRS VAN DAAN. *She then moves to the sink and inspects it.*)

Their son, Peter — my daughters, Margot and Anne.

(ANNE *gives a polite little curtsy as she shakes* MR VAN DAAN'S *hand. She puts her bag on the left end of the table C then immediately starts off on a tour of investigation of her new home, going upstairs to the attic room.*)

KRALER   I'm sorry there is still so much confusion.

MR FRANK   Please. Don't think of it. After all, we'll have plenty of leisure to arrange everything ourselves.

MIEP   (*indicating the sink cupboard*) We put the stores of food you sent in here. (*She crosses to the shelves.*) Your drugs are here — soap, linen, here.

MRS FRANK   Thank you, Miep.

MIEP   I made up the beds — the way Mr Frank and Mr Kraler said. Forgive me. I have to hurry. I've got to go to the other side of town to get some ration books for you.

MRS V. DAAN Ration books? If they see our names on ration books, they'll know we're here.

KRALER } (*together*) There isn't anything . . .

MIEP Don't worry. Your names won't be on them. (*As she hurries out.*) I'll be up later.

MR FRANK Thank you, Miep.

(MIEP *exits down the stairwell.*)

MRS FRANK It's illegal, then, the ration books? We've never done anything illegal.

MR FRANK We won't be living exactly according to regulations here.

KRALER This isn't the black market, Mrs Frank. This is what we call the white market – helping all of the hundreds and hundreds who are hiding out in Amsterdam.

(*The carillon is heard playing the quarter hour before eight.* KRALER *looks at his watch.* ANNE *comes down from the attic, stops at the window and looks out through the curtains.*)

ANNE It's the Westertoren.

KRALER I must go. I must be out of here and downstairs in the office before the workmen get here. Miep or I, or both of us, will be up each day to bring you food and news and find out what your needs are. Tomorrow I'll get you a better bolt for the door at the foot of the stairs. It needs a bolt that you can throw yourself and open only at our signal. (*To* MR FRANK.) Oh – you'll tell them about the noise?

MR FRANK   I'll tell them.

KRALER   Good-bye, then, for the moment. I'll come up again, after the workmen leave.

MR FRANK   (*shaking* KRALER'S *hand*) Good-bye, Mr Kraler.

MRS FRANK   (*shaking* KRALER'S *hand*) How can we thank you?

KRALER   I never thought I'd live to see the day when a man like Mr Frank would have to go into hiding. When you think . . .

(KRALER *breaks off and exits down the stairs.* MR FRANK *follows him down the stairs and bolts the door after him. In the interval before he returns,* PETER *goes to* MARGOT, *give a stiff bow and shakes hands with her.* ANNE *watches, and as they complete their greeting, moves to* PETER *and hold out her hand.* PETER *does not see her and turns away.* MR FRANK *comes up the stairs.*)

MRS FRANK   What did he mean, about the noise?

MR FRANK   First, let's take off some of these clothes.

(ANNE *moves below the table, stands with her back to the audience, removes her cape and beret and puts them on the pile of clothes on the table. They all start to take off garment after garment. On each of their coats, sweaters, blouses, suits and dresses is another yellow Star of David.* MR *and* MRS FRANK *are under-dressed quite simply. The others wear several things, sweaters, extra dresses, bathrobes, aprons, etc.* MRS FRANK *takes off her gloves, carefully folding them before putting them away.)*

MR V. DAAN   It's a wonder we weren't arrested, walking along the streets – Petronella with a fur coat in July – and that cat of Peter's crying all the way.

ANNE   (*removing a pair of panties*) A cat?

MRS FRANK   (*shocked*) Anne, please!

ANNE   It's all right. I've got on three more (*She removes two more pairs of panties. Finally, as they finish removing their surplus clothing, they settle down.*)

MR FRANK   Now. About the noise. While the men are in the building below, we must have complete quiet. Every sound can be heard down there, not only in the workrooms, but in the offices, too. The men come about eight-thirty, and leave at about five-thirty. So, to be perfectly safe, from eight in the morning until six in the evening we must move only when it is necessary and then in stockinged feet. We must not speak above a whisper. We must not run any water. We cannot use the sink, or even, forgive me, the WC. The pipes go down through the workrooms. It would be heard. No rubbish . . .

(*The sound of marching feet is heard.* MR FRANK, *followed by* ANNE, *peers out of the window. Satisfied that the marching feet are going away, he returns and continues.*)

No rubbish must ever be thrown out which might reveal that someone is living here – not even a potato paring.

We must burn everything in the stove at night. This is
the way we must live until it is over, if we are to survive.

(*There is a pause.* MARGOT *accidentally drops the
nightgown she is taking off.* PETER *jumps to pick it up
for her.*)

MRS FRANK   Until it is over.

MR FRANK   After six we can move about – we can talk and laugh
and have our supper and read and play games – just as
we would at home. (*He looks at his watch.*) And now I
think it would be wise if we all went to our rooms, and
were settled before eight o'clock. Mrs Van Dann, you
and your husband will go upstairs. I regret that there's
no place up there for Peter. But he will be here, near
us. This will be our common room, where we'll meet
to talk and eat and read, like one family.

MRS V. DAAN   And where do you and Mrs Frank sleep?

MR FRANK   This room is also our bedroom.

(MRS VAN DAAN *rises in protest.*)

MRS V. DAAN   That isn't right. We'll sleep here and
            } (*together*) you take the room upstairs. It's your
MR V. DAAN   place.

MR FRANK   Please. I've thought this out for weeks. It's the best
arrangement. The only arrangement.

(MR VAN DAAN *starts to load his arms with the clothes
he and his wife have taken off and thrown across the
couch.*)

MRS V. DAAN   (*shaking* MR FRANK'S *hand*) Never, never can we thank you. (*She moves to* MRS FRANK *and shakes her hand.*) I don't know what would have happened to us, if it hadn't been for Mr Frank.

MR FRANK   You don't know how your husband helped me when I came to this country – knowing no-one – not able to speak the language. I can never repay him for that. May I help you with your things?

MR V. DAAN   No. No. (*He picks up the carton and moves towards the attic stairs. To* MRS VAN DAAN) Come along, liefje.

MRS V. DAAN   You'll be all right, Peter? You're not afraid?

PETER   (*embarrassed*) Please, Mother. (*He picks up his gear.* MRS FRANK *goes to the head of the stairwell and stares thoughtfully down.* MR *and* MRS VAN DAAN *go upstairs.*)

MR FRANK   You, too, must have some rest, Edith. You didn't close your eyes last night. Nor you, Margot.

ANNE   I slept, Father. Wasn't that funny? I knew it was the last night in my own bed, and yet I slept soundly.

MR FRANK   I'm glad, Anne. Now you'll be able to help me straighten things in here. (*To* MRS FRANK *and* MARGOT.) Come with me – you and Margot rest in this room for the time being.

MRS FRANK   You're sure? I could help, really. And Anne hasn't had her milk.

MR FRANK　　I'll give it to her. (*He crosses to the table and picks up the pile of clothes.*) Anne, Peter – it's best that you take off your shoes now, before you forget. (*He leads the way to the room, goes in and switches on the pendant light.* MARGOT *goes into the room.* ANNE *and* PETER *remove their shoes.*)

MRS FRANK　　You're sure you're not tired, Anne?

ANNE　　I feel fine. I'm going to help father.

MRS FRANK　　Peter, I'm glad you are to be with us.

PETER　　Yes, Mrs Frank.

(MRS FRANK *goes into the room and closes the door. During the following scene* MR FRANK *helps* MARGOT *to hang up clothes.* PETER *takes his cat out of its case.*)

ANNE　　What's your cat's name?

PETER　　'Mouschi'.

ANNE　　Mouschi! Mouschi! Mouschi! (*She picks up the cat.*) I love cats. I have one – a darling little cat. But they made me leave her behind. I left some food and a note for the neighbours to take care of her – I'm going to miss her terribly. What is yours? A him or a her?

PETER　　He's a tom. He doesn't like strangers. (*He takes the cat from* ANNE, *and puts it back in its carrier.*)

ANNE　　Then I'll have to stop being a stranger, won't I? Is he fixed?

PETER   Huh?

ANNE   Did you have him altered?

PETER   No.

ANNE   Oh, you ought to – to keep him from fighting. Where did you go to school?

PETER   Jewish Secondary.

ANNE   But that's where Margot and I go. I never saw you around.

PETER   I used to see you – sometimes.

ANNE   You did?

PETER   In the school yard. You were always in the middle of a bunch of kids. (*He takes a penknife from his pocket.*)

ANNE   Why didn't you ever come over?

PETER   I'm sort of a lone wolf. (*He starts to rip off his Star of David.*)

ANNE   What are you doing?

PETER   Taking it off.

ANNE   But you can't do that. (*She grabs his hands and stops him.*) They'll arrest you if you go out without your star.

PETER   (*pulling away*) Who's going out? (*He crosses to the stove, lifts the lid and throws the star into the stove.*)

ANNE   Why, of course. You're right. Of course we don't need
them any more. (*She takes* PETER'S *knife and removes
her star.* PETER *waits for her star to throw it away.*)

I wonder what our friends will think when we don't
show up today?

PETER   I didn't have any dates with anyone.

ANNE   (*concentrating on her star*) Oh, I did. I had a date with
Jopie this afternoon to go and play ping-pong at her
house. Do you know Jopie de Waal?

PETER   No.

ANNE   Jopie's my best friend. I wonder what she'll think when
she telephones and there's no answer? Probably she'll
go over to the house – I wonder what she'll think – we
left everything as if we'd suddenly been called away –
breakfast dishes in the sink – beds not made . . . (*As she
pulls off her star, the cloth underneath shows clearly
the colour and form of the star.*) Look! It's still there.
What're you going to do with yours?

PETER   Burn it. (*He moves to the stove and holds out his hand
for* ANNE'S *star.* ANNE *starts to give the star to* PETER, *but
cannot.*)

ANNE   It's funny. I can't throw it away. I don't know why.

PETER   You can't throw . . .? Something they branded you with? That they made you wear so they could spit on you?

ANNE   I know. I know. But after all, it *is* the Star of David, isn't it?

(*The* VAN DAANS *have arranged their things, have put their clothes in the wardrobe and are sitting on the bed, fanning themselves.*)

PETER   Maybe it's different for a girl.

(ANNE *puts her star in her school bag.*)

MR FRANK   Forgive me, Peter. Now, let me see. We must find a bed for your cat. I'm glad you brought your cat. Anne was feeling so badly about hers.

(*He sees a small worn wash-tub and pulls it from the top shelf.*)

Here we are. Will it be comfortable in that?

PETER   Thanks.

MR FRANK   And here is your room. But I warn you, Peter, you can't grow any more. Not an inch, or you'll have to sleep with your feet out of the skylight. Are you hungry?

PETER   No.

MR FRANK   We have some bread and butter.

PETER   No, thank you.

MR FRANK   (*with a friendly pat on* PETER'S *shoulder*) You can have
            it for luncheon, then. And tonight we will have a real
            supper – our first supper together.

PETER   Thanks. Thanks. (*He goes into his room.* MR FRANK
            closes the door after PETER, *then sits and removes his
            shoes.*)

MR FRANK   That's a nice boy, Peter.

ANNE   He's awfully shy, isn't he?

MR FRANK   You'll like him, I know.

ANNE   I certainly hope so, since he's the only boy I'm likely to
            see for months and months.

MR FRANK   Anne, there's a box there. Will you open it?

            (*The sound of children playing is heard from the
            street below.* MR FRANK *goes to the sink and pours a
            glass of milk from the thermos bottle.*)

ANNE   You know the way I'm going to think of it here? I'm
            going to think of it as a boarding-house. A very peculiar
            Summer boarding-house, like the one that we ... (*She
            breaks off as she looks in the box.*) Father! Father! My
            film stars. I was wondering where they were – and
            Queen Wilhelmina. How wonderful!

MR FRANK   There's something more. Go on. Look further.

            (ANNE *digs deeper into the box and brings out a velour-
            covered book. She examines it in delighted silence for*

*a moment, then opens the cover slowly, and looks up
at* MR FRANK *with shining eyes.*)

ANNE   A diary! (*She throws her arms around him.*) I've never
had a diary. And I've always longed for one. (*She rushes
to the table and looks for a pencil.*) Pencil, pencil,
pencil, pencil. (*She darts across to the stair-well and
starts down the stairs.*) I'm going down to the office to
get a pencil.

MR FRANK   Anne! No! (*He strides to* ANNE *and catches her arm.*
MRS FRANK *aware of the sudden movement and sounds,
sits up. After a moment she rises, goes to the window
and looks out, then returns and sits on the bed.*)

ANNE   (*startled*) But there's no-one in the building now.

MR FRANK   It doesn't matter. I don't want you ever to go beyond
that door.

ANNE   (*sobered*) Never? Not even at night time, when
everyone is gone? Or on Sundays? Can't I go down to
listen to the radio?

MR FRANK   Never. I am sorry, Anneke. It isn't safe. No, you must
never go beyond that door.

ANNE   I see. (*For the first time she realizes what 'going into
hiding' means.*)

MR FRANK   It'll be hard, I know. But always remember this,
Anneke. There are no walls, there are no bolts, no locks
that anyone can put on your mind. Miep will bring us
books. We will read history, poetry, mythology. (*He
gives* ANNE *the glass of milk.*) Here's your milk.

(MR FRANK *puts his arm about* ANNE, *and crosses with her to the couch, where they sit side by side.*)

As a matter of fact, between us, Annie, being here has certain advantages for you. For instance you remember the battle you had with your mother the other day on the subject of goloshes? You said you'd rather die than wear goloshes. But in the end you had to wear them. Well now, you see for as long as we are here you will never have to wear goloshes. Isn't that good? And the coat that you inherited from Margot –

(ANNE *makes a wry face.*)

– you won't have to wear that. And the piano. You won't have to practise on the piano. I tell you, this is going to be a fine life for you.

(ANNE'S *panic is gone.* PETER *appears in the doorway of his room, with a saucer in one hand and the cat in the other.*)

PETER   I – I – I thought I'd better get some water for Mouschi before . . .

MR FRANK   Of course.

(*The carillon begins its melody and strikes eight. As it does so,* MR FRANK *motions for* PETER *and* ANNE *to be quiet, tiptoes to the window in the rear wall and peers down.* MR VAN DAAN *rises and moves to the head of the attic stairs.* MR FRANK *puts his finger to his lips, indicating to* ANNE *and* PETER *that they must be silent, then steps down towards* PETER *indicating he can draw no water.* PETER *starts back to his room.* ANNE *rises and crosses below the table to* PETER. MR FRANK *crosses quietly towards the girls' room. As* PETER *reaches the door of his room*

*a board creaks under his foot. The three are frozen for
a minute in fear.* ANNE *then continues over to* PETER *on
tiptoe and pours some milk in the saucer.* PETER *squats
on the floor, putting the milk down before the cat and
encouraging him to drink.* MR FRANK *crosses to them,
gives* ANNE *his fountain pen, then crosses to the girls'
room, goes inside, sits on the bed and puts a
comforting arm around* MRS FRANK. ANNE *squats for a
moment beside* PETER, *watching the cat, then opens her
diary and writes. All are silent and motionless, except*
MR VAN DAAN *who returns to* MRS VAN DAAN *and fans her
with a newspaper. The Westertoren finishes tolling the
hour. As* ANNE *begins to write, her voice is heard faintly
at first, then with growing strength.*)

ANNE   I expect I should be describing what it feels like to go
         into hiding. But I really don't know yet, myself. I only
         know it's funny never to be able to go outdoors –
         never to breathe fresh air – never to run and shout and
         jump. It's the silence in the night that frightens me
         most. Every time I hear a creak in the house, or a step
         on the street outside, I'm sure they're coming for us.
         The days aren't so bad. At least we know that Miep and
         Mr Kraler are down there below us in the office. Our
         protectors, we call them. I asked father what would
         happen to them if the Nazis found out they were hiding
         us. Pim said that they would suffer the same fate that
         we would. Imagine! They know this and yet when they
         come up here, they're always cheerful and gay as if
         there were nothing in the world to bother them.
         Friday, the twenty-first of August, nineteen forty-two.
         Today I'm going to tell you our general news. Mother
         is unbearable. She insists on treating me like a baby,
         which I loathe. Otherwise things are going better. The
         weather is . . .

Scene Three

The same. August 1942. A few minutes after six p.m.

MR FRANK, *with his shoes in his hand, is standing at the window looking down at the street below, waiting to see that the workmen have left the building. The group in the room watch him intently, waiting for his signal to be able to move.* MRS VAN DAAN *sits in the chair above the stair-well, her fur coat in her lap.* ANNE *and* PETER *are seated opposite each other at the table, where they have been doing lessons in copybooks.* MRS FRANK *stands above the couch, shoes in hand, waiting to put them on.* MARGOT *is seated at the dressing-table in her room, where she is studying.* MR VAN DAAN *is in the attic room, playing solitaire on the bed. From outside we hear the sounds of street traffic and the distant ships' sirens. After a couple of seconds of silence,* MR FRANK *turns from the window.*

MR FRANK   (*to the group quietly*) It's safe now. The last workman has left.

(*There is an immediate stir of relief and activity among the people in the main room.*)

ANNE   (*throwing her arms and legs wide in an exaggerated gesture of relief*) Whee! (*She rises.*)

MRS FRANK   (*startled and amused*) Anne!

MRS V. DAAN   (*rising*) I'm first for the WC.

(MRS VAN DAAN *hurries across and goes into the WC, pausing only long enough to drape her coat carefully over the chair. Inside the WC she turns on the light.*

(MRS FRANK *puts on her shoes and goes to the sink to prepare supper. She puts on her apron and begins beating a bowl of batter.* ANNE *sneaks* PETER'S *shoes from under the table as he stretches, and hides them behind her back.* MR FRANK, *carrying his shoes, goes into the girls' room.*)

MR FRANK   (*to* MARGOT) Six o'clock. School's over. (*He sits and puts on his shoes.* MARGOT *rises and stretches. In the centre room* ANNE *is watching as* PETER *tries to find his shoes. He remains seated as he peers under the table.*)

PETER   (*to* ANNE) Have you seen my shoes?

ANNE   (*innocently*) Your shoes?

PETER   You've taken them, haven't you?

ANNE   I don't know what you're talking about.

PETER   You're going to be sorry.

ANNE   Am I? (*She holds the shoes tightly and makes a feint as if to run. She hides behind* MRS FRANK *but* PETER *manages to catch her hands. They struggle and fall to the floor.*)

MRS FRANK   (*protesting*) Anne, dear!

PETER   Wait till I get you.

ANNE   I'm waiting.

(PETER *pins* ANNE *down, wrestling to get the shoes.*)

Don't! Don't! Peter, stop it. Ouch!

MRS FRANK Anne! Peter!

(PETER *suddenly becomes self-conscious, roughly grabs his shoes and moves towards his room.*)

ANNE (*catching* PETER) Peter, where are you going? Come, dance with me.

PETER I tell you I don't know how.

ANNE I'll teach you.

PETER I'm going to give Mouschi his dinner.

ANNE Can I watch?

PETER He doesn't like people around while he eats.

ANNE Peter, please.

PETER No. (*He goes into the room.* ANNE *slams the door after* PETER.)

MRS FRANK Anne, dear, I think you shouldn't play like that with Peter. It's not dignified.

(ANNE *is now deflated and inspecting her chafed elbows.*)

ANNE Who cares if it's dignified? I don't want to be dignified.

(*She throws herself across the chair in a most undignified manner.* MR FRANK *turns off the table-lamp.* MARGOT *gives him her copybook. They come into the centre room.* MARGOT *moves to help* MRS FRANK.

MR FRANK *moves below the table and gathers up* ANNE'S *copybooks.* PETER, *in his room, puts on his shoes.*)

MRS FRANK You complain that I don't treat you like a grown-up. But when I do, you resent it.

(MARGOT *brings a cloth and wipes the table.*)

ANNE I only want some fun – someone to laugh and clown with. After you've sat still all day and hardly moved, you've got to have some fun. I don't know what's the matter with that boy.

MR FRANK He isn't used to girls. Give him a little time.

ANNE Time? Isn't two months time? I could cry. Come on, Margot – dance with me. Come on, please.

MARGOT (*pulling away*) I have to help with supper. (*She returns to her duties with* MRS FRANK.)

ANNE You know we're going to forget how to dance. When we get out we won't remember a thing. (*She sings to herself, and waltzes.* MR FRANK *is looking at* PETER'S *copybook. As* ANNE *approaches he holds out his arms and they do a few turns of a waltz.*)

MRS V. DAAN (*as she enters*) Next? (*She looks around as she starts putting on her shoes.*) Where's Peter?

ANNE Where would he be?

(MR FRANK *and* ANNE *finish with a flourish and a bow.* ANNE *continues singing quietly.*)

MRS V. DAAN   He hasn't finished his lessons, has he? His father'll kill him if he catches him in there with that cat and his work not done. Anne, get him out of there, will you?

(ANNE *dances quickly to* PETER'S *door and knocks in rhythm to her singing.*)

ANNE   Peter. Peter.

PETER   (*opening the door*) What is it?

ANNE   Your mother says to come out.

PETER   I'm giving Mouschi his dinner.

MRS V. DAAN   You know what your father says. (*She arranges the coat carefully over her lap, caressing the fur and touching her cheek with the collar.*)

PETER   For Heaven's sake, I haven't even looked at him since lunch.

MRS V. DAAN   I'm just telling you, that's all.

ANNE   I'll feed him.

PETER   I don't want you in there.

MRS V. DAAN   Peter!

PETER   (*to* ANNE) Then give him his dinner and come right out, you hear?

(ANNE *goes into* PETER'S *room, closes the door and disappears behind the curtain covering his closet.*)

MRS V. DAAN   (*to* PETER) Now, is that any way to talk to your little girl friend?

PETER   Mother – for Heaven's sake – will you please stop saying that?

MRS V. DAAN   Look at him blush. Look at him.

PETER   (*uncomfortable*) Please. I'm not – anyway – let me alone, will you?

MRS V. DAAN   He acts like it was something to be ashamed of. It's nothing to be ashamed of, to have a little girl friend.

PETER   You're crazy. She's only thirteen.

MRS V. DAAN   So what? And you're sixteen. Just perfect. Your father's ten years older than I am. (*To* MR FRANK.) I warn you, Mr Frank, if this war lasts much longer, you and I are going to be related.

MR FRANK   Mazeltov!

MRS FRANK   I wonder where Miep is? She's usually so prompt.

(*Suddenly everything else is forgotten as they listen to a sound in the street. It is the sound of an automobile coming to a sudden stop. The people in the room are tense, motionless in their terror. The car starts away. A wave of relief sweeps over the people.* MRS FRANK *returns to her dinner preparations.* MR

FRANK *goes back to the copybooks.* ANNE *suddenly flings open the door of the room, and makes a dramatic entrance. She is dressed in* PETER'S *'plus-fours', jacket and cap. She affects a long stride and a deep voice.* PETER *looks at her in fury. The others are amused.*)

ANNE   Good evening, everyone. Forgive me if I don't stay. I have a friend waiting for me in there. My friend Tom – Tom Cat. (*She hops on to the chair above the table and puts one foot on the table.*) Some people say that we look alike. But Tom has the most beautiful whiskers – (*she strokes her imaginary whiskers.* PETER *rises.*)

– and I have only a little fuzz. I am hoping – in time . . .

PETER   All right, Mrs Quack Quack.

ANNE   (*jumping down and pushing* PETER *away; outraged*) Peter!

PETER   I heard about you – how you talked so much in class they called you 'Mrs Quack Quack'. (*He moves below the table and picks up his copybook.*) How Mr Smitter made you write a composition – '"Quack quack", said Mrs Quack Quack.'

ANNE   Well, go on. Tell them the rest. (ANNE *pursues* PETER *and gives him another shove as he picks up the book. She uses both hands and the trousers fall to her ankles. She hitches them up and continues after* PETER.)

How it was so good he read it out loud to the class and then read it to all his other classes.

PETER   Quack! Quack! Quack-quack-quack.

ANNE   (*pulling off the coat and trousers*) You are the most intolerable, insufferable boy I've ever met. (*She throws the clothes down the stair-well.*)

MRS V. DAAN   That's right, Anneke. Give it to him.

ANNE   (*slumping in the chair above the stairwell*) With all the boys in the world – why I had to get locked up with one like you.

PETER   (*coming up the stairs*) Quack, quack, quack, and from now on stay out of my room. (*He turns towards his room.* ANNE *puts out her foot and trips* PETER, *who picks himself up, furious and inarticulate, and takes the clothes into his closet. The door is left open.* ANNE *is all innocence.* MRS FRANK *moves to* ANNE *and smooths her hair. In doing so she feels* ANNE'S *forehead.*)

MRS FRANK   (*quietly*) Anne, dear – your hair. You're warm. Are you feeling all right?

ANNE   Please, Mother. (*She slips her feet into her shoes.*)

MRS FRANK   You haven't a fever, have you?

ANNE   No. No.

MRS FRANK   Anneke, dear, don't do that. You know we can't call a doctor here, ever. There's only one thing to do – watch carefully. Prevent an illness before it comes.

(ANNE *turns her back.*)

Let me see your tongue.

ANNE   Mother, this is perfectly absurd.

MRS FRANK   Anne, dear, don't be such a baby. Let me see your tongue.

(ANNE *shakes her head.*)

Otto . . .?

MR FRANK   You hear your mother, Anne.

(ANNE *turns her head towards her mother, sticks out her tongue for an instant, and immediately turns away.*)

MRS FRANK   (*good-naturedly*) Come on – open up.

(ANNE, *since she must, goes all the way and puts out her tongue as far as possible, and with her mouth wide open, leans towards her mother.*)

You seem all right – but perhaps an aspirin . . .

(*She returns to the sink.* ANNE *follows* MRS FRANK *to the sink.* MRS VAN DAAN *moves and stands above the table.* MR VAN DAAN, *in the attic, puts away his cards and comes down the stairs.*)

MRS V. DAAN   For Heaven's sake don't give that child any pills. I waited for fifteen minutes this morning for her to come out of the WC.

ANNE   I was washing my hair.

MR FRANK   I think there's nothing the matter with our Anne that a ride on her bike, or a visit with Jopie de Waal wouldn't cure. Isn't that so, Anne?

(ANNE *moves to* MR FRANK *and gives him a hug.* MR VAN DAAN *crosses to* MRS VAN DAAN. *The sound of a fleet of bombers is heard high overhead, along with bursts of ack-ack fire. This continues for some time.*)

MR V. DAAN   Miep not come yet?

MRS V. DAAN   The workmen just left, a little while ago.

MR V. DAAN   What's for dinner tonight?

MRS V. DAAN   Beans.

MR V. DAAN   Not again!

MRS V. DAAN   Poor Putti! I know. But what can we do? That's all that Miep brought us.

(MR VAN DAAN *resumes his pacing.* ANNE *moves quickly behind him and follows him, imitating his posture and stride.*)

ANNE   (*in a deep voice*) We are now in what is known as the 'bean cycle'. Beans boiled, beans en casserole, beans with strings, beans without strings . . .

(PETER *starts out with his copybook.*)

MR V. DAAN   (*to* PETER) I saw you – in there, playing with your cat.

(MRS VAN DAAN *spreads her coat across her lap and strokes the fur.*)

MRS V. DAAN   He just went in for a second, putting his coat away. He's been out here all the time, doing his lessons.

MR FRANK   Anne, you got an excellent in your history paper today – and very good in Latin.

ANNE   How about algebra?

MR FRANK   I'll have to make a confession. Up until now I've managed to stay ahead of you in algebra. Today you caught up with me. We'll leave it to Margot to correct.

ANNE   Isn't algebra *vile*, Pim?

MR FRANK   Vile!

MARGOT   How did I do?

ANNE   Excellent, excellent, excellent, excellent!

MR FRANK   (*to* MARGOT) You should have used the subjunctive here.

MARGOT   Should I? I thought – look here – I didn't use it here ...

(MARGOT *and* MR FRANK *become absorbed in the copybooks.*)

ANNE   Mrs Van Daan, may I try on your coat?

MRS FRANK   No, Anne.

(MRS VAN DAAN *holds up the coat so that* ANNE *can slip into it.*)

MRS V. DAAN   It's all right – but be careful with it. My father gave me that the year before he died. He always bought the best that money could buy.

ANNE   Mrs Van Daan, did you have a lot of boyfriends before you were married?

MRS FRANK   Anne, that's a personal question. It's not courteous to ask personal questions.

MRS V. DAAN   Oh, I don't mind.

(*To* ANNE) Our house was always swarming with boys. When I was a girl we had . . .

MR V. DAAN   Oh, God! Not again . . .

MRS V. DAAN   (*good-humouredly*) Shut up! (*She continues without a pause to* ANNE.) One summer we had a big house in Hilversum. The boys came buzzing around like bees around a jam pot. And when I was sixteen – we were wearing our skirts very short those days and I had good-looking legs. (*Stands by* MR FRANK. *She is very flirtatious.*) I still have 'em. I may not be as pretty as I used to be, but I still have my legs. (*She pulls up her skirt to above her knees.* MR FRANK *is a bit nonplussed as he looks up and sees* MRS VAN DAAN.)

How about it, Mr Frank?

MR V. DAAN   All right. All right. We see them.

MRS V. DAAN   I'm not asking you. I'm asking Mr Frank.

PETER   Mother, for Heaven's sake . . .!

MRS V. DAAN   Oh, I embarrass you, do I? Well, I just hope the girl you
marry has as good. (*To* ANNE.) My father used to worry
about me, with so many boys hanging round. He told
me, if any of them gets fresh, you say to him (*She
places one hand on* ANNE'S *shoulder and with the other
holds up a warning finger.*)

'Remember, Mr So-and-So, remember I'm a lady.' (*She
gives* ANNE *a little tap on the cheek.*)

ANNE   (*imitating the action and delivery of* MRS VAN DAAN)
'Remember, Mr So-and-So, remember I'm a lady.'

(MRS VAN DAAN *takes the coat from* ANNE, *who sprawls
on her stomach on the floor. Her legs are spread wide
as she listens for sounds below with an ear pressed to
the boards.*)

MR V. DAAN   (*to his wife*) Look at you, talking that way in front of
her. Don't you know she puts it all down in her diary?

MRS V. DAAN   So if she does? I'm only telling the truth.

(MRS FRANK *collects a tablecloth from the shelves and
moves above the table.* MARGOT *takes all the books
from* MR FRANK, *crosses and puts them on the
mantelpiece, then goes to the shelves and collects
seven plates.*)

MRS FRANK   Would you mind Peter, if I moved you over to the
couch?

ANNE   (*listening*) Miep must have the radio on.

MR V. DAAN   (*confronting* PETER) Haven't you finished yet?

PETER   No.

MR V. DAAN   You ought to be ashamed of yourself. (*He paces and is irritated when he has to step over one of* ANNE'S *widespread legs. The sound of the aircraft and ack-ack fades.*)

PETER   All right. All right. I'm a dunce. I'm a hopeless case. Why do I go on?

(MRS FRANK *spreads the tablecloth.* MARGOT *brings the plates and puts them on the table, then goes and collects knives and forks.*)

MRS V. DAAN   (*to* PETER) You're not hopeless. Don't talk that way. It's just that you haven't anyone to help you, like the girls have. (*To* MR FRANK.) Maybe you could help him, Mr Frank?

MR FRANK   I'm sure that his father . . .

MR V. DAAN   Not me. I can't do anything with him. He won't listen to me. You go ahead – if you want.

MR FRANK   What about it, Peter? Shall we make our school co-educational?

MRS V. DAAN   You're an angel, Mr Frank. An angel! (*She takes* MR FRANK'S *face in her hands and kisses him on the mouth.*) I don't know why I didn't meet you before I met – (*She indicates* MR VAN DAAN.) that one there. Here, sit down, Mr Frank. Now, Peter, you listen to Mr Frank.

MR FRANK   (*uncomfortable*) It might be better for us to go into Peter's room.

MRS V. DAAN   That's right. You go in there, Peter. You listen to Mr Frank. Mr Frank is a highly educated man.

(MR FRANK *rises and follows* PETER. MRS FRANK *intercepts him and wipes the lipstick from his lips.* PETER *goes into his room.* MR FRANK, *embarrassed, hurries in after* PETER. *During the following scene he and* PETER *sit on the bed and* MR FRANK *helps* PETER *with his lessons.*)

ANNE   (*listening*) Shh! I can hear a man's voice talking.

MR V. DAAN   (*to* ANNE) Isn't it bad enough here without your sprawling all over the place?

(ANNE *scrambles to a sitting position, with her back against the table.*)

MRS V. DAAN   (*to her husband*) If you didn't smoke so much, you wouldn't be so bad-tempered.

MR V. DAAN   Am I smoking? Do you see me smoking?

MRS V. DAAN   Don't tell me you've used up all those cigarettes?

MR V. DAAN   One package! Miep only brought me one package.

MRS V. DAAN   It's a filthy habit, anyway. It's a good time to break
yourself.

MR V. DAAN   Oh, stop it, please!

MRS V. DAAN   You're smoking up all our money. You know that, don't
you?

(MRS FRANK *and* MARGOT *studiously keep their eyes
down, but* ANNE, *seated on the floor, follows the
discussion interestedly.*)

MR V. DAAN   Will you shut up? (*He turns to see* ANNE *staring up at
him.*) And what are you staring at?

ANNE   I never heard grown-ups quarrel before. I thought only
children quarrelled.

MR V. DAAN   This isn't a quarrel. It's a discussion. And I never heard
children so rude before.

ANNE   I – rude?

MRS FRANK   Anne, will you bring me my knitting?

(ANNE *picks up the knitting.*)

I must remember, when Miep comes, to ask her to
bring me some more wool.

MARGOT   I need some hairpins and some soap. I made a list. (*She
goes into her room.* MARGOT *turns on the table-lamp
and writes out her list at the dressing-table.*)

MRS FRANK   (*to* ANNE) Have you some library books for Miep when
             she comes?

ANNE   (*handing the knitting to* MRS FRANK) It's a wonder that
             Miep has a life of her own the way we make her run
             errands for us. 'Please, Miep, get me some starch.'
             'Please take my hair out and have it cut.' 'Tell me all
             the latest news, Miep.' Did you know she was engaged?
             His name is Dirk and Miep's afraid the Nazis will ship
             him off to Germany to work in one of their war plants.
             That's what they're doing with some of the young
             Dutchmen – they pick them up off the streets . . .

MR V. DAAN   Don't you ever get tired of talking? Suppose you try
             keeping still for five minutes. Just five minutes.

             (ANNE *clamps her lips tight, rises, and strides behind*
             MR VAN DAAN, *mimicking him. As she passes* MRS FRANK,
             she jumps up, takes ANNE *by the arm and detours her
             to the sink.*)

MRS FRANK   Come here, Anne. Finish your glass of milk. (*She gives
             a glass of milk to* ANNE, *then sits above the table and
             knits.*)

MR V. DAAN   Talk, talk, talk. I never heard such a child. Where is
             my . . .? Every evening it's the same, talk, talk, talk.
             Where the . . .?

MRS V. DAAN What're you looking for?

MR V. DAAN   My pipe. Have you seen my pipe?

MRS V. DAAN What good's a pipe? You haven't got any tobacco.

MR V. DAAN   At least I'll have something to hold in my mouth. (*He opens* MARGOT'S *door and sticks his head in.*) Margot, have you seen my pipe?

(ANNE, *behind* MR VAN DAAN'S *back, steals to the table, places the glass of milk on it and snatches up his pipe. She then retreats up RC with lips still clamped and hiding the pipe behind her back.*)

MARGOT   It was on the table last night.

MR V. DAAN   I know. I know. Anne, did you see my pipe?

(ANNE *does not reply.*)

Anne!

MRS FRANK   Anne, dear, Mr Van Daan is speaking to you.

ANNE   (*feigning surprise; through tight lips*) Am I allowed to talk now?

MR V. DAAN   You're the most aggravating ... (*He controls himself with difficulty.*) The trouble with you is, you've been spoiled. What you need is a good old-fashioned spanking.

ANNE   (*mimicking* MRS VAN DAAN) 'Remember Mr So-and-So, remember I'm a lady.' (*She thrusts the pipe into* MR VAN DAAN'S *mouth, then picks up her glass of milk.*)

MR V. DAAN   Why aren't you nice and quiet like your sister Margot? Why do you have to show off all the time?

(ANNE *moves, trying to get around* MR VAN DAAN, *but he retreats, blocking her way.*)

Let me give you a little advice, young lady. Men don't like that kind of thing in a girl. You know that? A man likes a girl who'll listen to him once in a while – a domestic girl, who'll keep her house shining for her husband – who loves to cook and sew and . . .

ANNE   I'd cut my throat first. I'd open my veins. I'm going to be remarkable. I'm going to Paris.

MR V. DAAN   Paris!

ANNE   To study music and art.

MR V. DAAN   Yeah – yeah.

ANNE   I'm going to be a famous dancer or singer – or something wonderful. (*Arms held wide, milk in her right hand, she makes a dancer's turn. The milk spills over the fur coat on* MRS VAN DAAN'S *lap.* MRS VAN DAAN *is shocked and stunned.* ANNE *falls to her knees and tries to brush the milk away.* MARGOT *hurries down to them with a tea towel.*)

MRS V. DAAN   (*scarcely able to speak*) Now look what you've done – you clumsy little fool. My beautiful fur coat my father gave me.

ANNE   I'm so sorry.

MRS V. DAAN   What do you care? It isn't yours – so go on, ruin it. Do you know what that coat cost? Do you? And now look at it. Look at it.

ANNE   I'm very, very sorry.

MRS V. DAAN   I could kill you for this. I could just kill you. (*She goes up the stairs, clutching her coat.*)

MR V. DAAN   (*following his wife*) Petronella – liefje – come back – the supper – come back. (*He goes up into the attic.*)

MRS FRANK   Anne, you mustn't behave in that way.

(MARGOT *returns to the sink, taking the glass and cloth with her.*)

ANNE   (*still kneeling*) It was an accident. Anyone can have an accident.

MRS FRANK   I don't mean that. I mean the answering back. You must not answer back.

(ANNE *rises and walks heel-to-toe along a crack in the floor.*)

They are our guests. We must always show the greatest courtesy to them. We're all living under terrible tension. That's why we must control ourselves. You don't hear Margot getting into arguments with them, do you? Watch Margot. She's always courteous with them. Never familiar. She keeps her distance. And they respect her for it. Try to be like Margot.

ANNE   And have them walk all over me, the way they do her? No, thanks.

MRS FRANK   I'm not afraid that anyone is going to walk all over you, Anne. I'm afraid for other people, that you'll walk on them. I don't know what happens to you, Anne. You are wild, self-willed. If I had ever talked to my mother as you talk to me ...

ANNE   Things have changed. People aren't like that any more. 'Yes, Mother.' 'No, Mother.' 'Anything you say, Mother.' I've got to fight things out for myself. Make something of myself. (*She turns away.*)

MRS FRANK   It isn't necessary to fight to do it. Margot doesn't fight, and isn't she . . .?

ANNE   (*wheeling on her mother; violently rebellious*) Margot! Margot! Margot! That's all I hear from everyone – how wonderful Margot is – 'Why aren't you like Margot?'

MARGOT   Oh, come on, Anne, don't be so . . .

ANNE   (*paying no attention*) Everything she does is right, and everything I do is wrong. I'm the goat around here. You're all against me – and you worst of all. (*She rushes off into her room and throws herself down on the chaise-longue, stifling her sobs.* MRS FRANK *sighs, rises, crosses and puts her knitting on the mantelpiece.*)

MRS FRANK   Let's put the soup on the stove – if there's anyone who cares to eat. Margot, will you take the bread out?

(MARGOT *takes the bread from the sink cupboard.*)

I don't know how we can go on living this way – I can't say a word to Anne – she flies at me.

MARGOT   You know Anne. (*She takes a bread plate from the shelves.*) In half-an-hour she'll be out here, laughing and joking.

MRS FRANK   And – (*she makes a motion upwards, indicating the*
             VAN DAANS) I told your father it wouldn't work – but no
             – no – he had to ask them, he said – he owed it to him,
             he said. Well, he knows now that I was right. These
             quarrels – this bickering . . .

MARGOT   (*placing the bread on the table; with a warning look*)
             Shush! Shush!

             (*The buzzer for the door sounds. The buzzer signal
             used by* MIEP *and* KRALER *is always the International
             Code 'V'. Dit-dit-dit-dah.* MRS FRANK, *startled, gasps.*)

MRS FRANK   Every time I hear that sound my heart stops.

MARGOT   It's Miep. (*She knocks at* PETER'S *door.*) Father.

             (*The attic light is switched off.* MR FRANK *rises, comes
             quickly from* PETER'S *room and hurries down the stair-
             well.*)

MR FRANK   (*as he goes*) Thank you, Margot. Has everyone his list?

MARGOT   I'll get my books. (*She indicates to* MRS FRANK *the list
             on the table.*) Here's your list. (*She goes into her room.*
             MRS FRANK *goes to the table and collects the list.* ANNE
             sits up, hiding her tears.)

             (*to* ANNE) Miep's here. (*She picks up her books and
             returns to the centre room.* ANNE *rises, looks in the
             mirror and smooths her hair.* MR VAN DAAN *comes
             down from the attic.*)

MR V. DAAN   Is it Miep?

MARGOT   Yes. Father's gone down to let her in.

MR V. DAAN   At last I'll have some cigarettes.

MRS FRANK   I can't tell you how unhappy I am about Mrs Van
Daan's coat. Anne should never have touched it.

MR V. DAAN   She'll be all right.

MRS FRANK   Is there anything I can do?

MR V. DAAN   Don't worry. (*He turns towards the stairwell.* KRALER
and MR FRANK *come up the stairwell. Their faces are
grave.* ANNE *and* PETER *come from their rooms.*)

MRS FRANK   Mr Kraler!

(*The sound of a streetcar is heard.*)

MR V. DAAN   (*shaking* KRALER'S *hand*) How are you, Mr Kraler?

MARGOT   This is a surprise.

MRS FRANK   When Mr Kraler comes the sun begins to shine.

MR V. DAAN   Miep is coming?

KRALER   Not tonight.

MRS FRANK   (*to* KRALER) Wouldn't you like a cup of coffee – or,
better still, will you have supper with us?

KRALER   No, thank you.

MR FRANK   Mr Kraler has something to talk over with us.
Something has happened, he says, which demands an
immediate decision.

MRS FRANK   (*fearfully*) What is it?

(KRALER *crosses to the couch, sits, opens his brief-case
and takes out a quart bottle of milk, two cabbages
and a loaf of bread. He gives the food to* MARGOT *and*
ANNE, *who put it in the sink cupboard.*)

KRALER   Usually, when I come up here, I try to bring you some
bit of good news. What's the use of telling you the bad
news when there's nothing that you can do about it?
But today something has happened. Dirk – Miep's Dirk,
you know, came to me just now. He tells me that he
has a Jewish friend living near him. A dentist. He says
he's in trouble. He begged me, could I do anything for
this man – could I find him a hiding place? So I've
come to you. I know it's a terrrible thing to ask of you,
living as you are, but would you take him in with you?

MR FRANK   Of course we will.

KRALER   It'll be just for a night or two – until I find some other
place. This happened so suddenly that I didn't know
where to turn.

MR FRANK   Where is he?

KRALER   Downstairs in the office.

MR FRANK   Good. Bring him up.

KRALER   His name is Dussel – Jan Dussel.

MR FRANK   Dussel – I think I know him.

KRALER   I'll get him.

(KRALER *exits quickly down the stairwell.* MR FRANK *suddenly becomes conscious of the others.*)

MR FRANK   Forgive me. I spoke without consulting you. But I knew you'd feel as I do.

MR V. DAAN   There's no reason for you to consult anyone. This is your place. You have a right to do exactly as you please. The only thing I feel – there's so little food as it is – and to take in another person . . .

(PETER, *ashamed of his father, turns away.*)

MR FRANK   We can stretch the food a little. It's only for a few days.

MR V. DAAN   You want to make a bet?

MRS FRANK   I think it's fine to have him. But, Otto, where are you going to put him? Where?

PETER   He can have my bed. I can sleep on the floor. I wouldn't mind.

MR FRANK   That's good of you, Peter. But your room's too small, even for *you*.

(*The sound of marching feet is heard off.* PETER *moves to the window and looks out.*)

ANNE   I have a much better idea. I'll come in here with you
       and mother, and Margot can take Peter's room and
       Peter can go in our room with Mr Dussel.

MARGOT   That's right. We could do that.

MR FRANK   No, Margot. You mustn't sleep in that room – neither
           you nor Anne. Mouschi has caught some rats in there.
           Peter's brave. He doesn't mind.

ANNE   Then how about *this*? I'll come in here with you and
       mother and Mr Dussel can have my bed.

MRS FRANK   No. Margot will come in here with us and he can have
            her bed. It's the only way. Margot, bring your things in
            here. Help her, Anne.

           (MARGOT *hurries into her room to collect her things.*
           PETER *moves to assist* MARGOT.)

ANNE   (*to* MRS FRANK; *rebelliously*) Why Margot? Why can't I
       come in here?

MRS FRANK   Because, it wouldn't be proper for Margot to sleep with
            a . . . Please, Anne. Don't argue. Please.

MR FRANK   (*to* ANNE) You don't mind sharing your room with Mr
           Dussel, do you, Anne?

ANNE   (*hiding her hurt*) No. No, of course not.

MR FRANK   Good. Where's the cognac?

MRS FRANK   (*indicating the shelves up L*) It's there. But, Otto, I was
            saving it in case of illness.

MR FRANK　　I think we couldn't find a better time to use it. Peter, will you get five glasses for me? (*He collects the bottle from the shelves.* PETER *collects five glasses from the shelf over the sink, puts them on the table.* MR FRANK *gives the bottle to* MRS FRANK *who pours a swallow into each glass.*)

MRS V. DAAN　　What's happening? What's going on?

MR V. DAAN　　Someone's moving in with us.

MRS V. DAAN　　In here? You're joking.

MARGOT　　It's only for a night or two – until Mr Kraler finds him another place.

MR V. DAAN　　Yeah! Yeah!

(KRALER *comes up the stairwell.* MR DUSSEL *follows him up. He is a man in his fifties, meticulous and finicky, but at the moment, bewildered. He carries a brief-case and a shopping bag, stuffed full, and has a small medicine case tucked under his arm. He wears a raincoat and hat.* MR FRANK *hurries to the stairwell and holds out his hand.* ANNE, *all eyes, sits above the table.*)

MR FRANK　　Come in, Mr Dussel.

KRALER　　This is Mr Frank.

DUSSEL　　Mr Otto Frank?

MR FRANK　　Yes. Let me take your things.

(MR FRANK *takes the hat and bags and hands them to*
PETER. DUSSEL *clings to his medicine case.*)

This is my wife, Edith – and Mrs Van Daan, and Mr Van
Daan – their son, Peter – and my daughters, Margot
and Anne.

(DUSSEL *shakes hands with everyone, crossing to the*
VAN DAANS.)

KRALER   Thank you, Mr Frank. Thank you all, Mr Dussel, I leave
you in good hands. Oh – Dirk's coat . . .

(DUSSEL *takes off his coat. Underneath is his white*
office jacket, with a yellow Star of David on it.)

DUSSEL   (*to* KRALER) What can I say to thank you? (*He hands the*
coat to KRALER.)

MRS FRANK   (*rising and handing drinks to the* VAN DAANS; *to*
DUSSEL) Mr Kraler and Miep – they're our life-line.
Without them we couldn't live.

(DUSSEL *sinks on to the chair.*)

KRALER   Please. Please. You make us seem very heroic. It isn't
that at all.

(MRS FRANK *offers a drink to* KRALER, *who refuses it, so*
she places it before DUSSEL. MR FRANK *moves and stands*
above DUSSEL. MARGOT *goes into her room, straightens*
the beds and sees that all is orderly.)

We simply don't like the Nazis. We don't like their
methods. We don't like anything about them.

MR FRANK   (*smiling*) I know. I know. 'No-one's going to tell us
            Dutchmen what to do with our damn Jews.'

KRALER   (*to* DUSSEL) Pay no attention to Mr Frank. I'll be up
            tomorrow to see that they're treating you right. (*To* MR
            FRANK.) Don't trouble to come down again. Peter will
            bolt the door after me, won't you, Peter?

PETER   (*moving quickly*) Yes, sir.

MR FRANK   Thank you, Peter. I'll do it.

KRALER   Good night. Good night.

ALL   (*ad lib*) Good night, Mr Kraler. See you tomorrow, etc.
            etc.

            (DUSSEL *rises.* KRALER *and* MR FRANK *exit down the stair-
            well.*)

MRS FRANK   Please, Mr Dussel, sit down.

DUSSEL   I'm dreaming. I know it. I can't believe my eyes. Mr
            Otto Frank, here. (*To* MRS FRANK.) You're not in
            Switzerland, then? A woman told me . . . She said she'd
            gone to your house – the door was open, everything
            was in disorder, dishes in the sink. She said she found a
            piece of paper in the waste basket with an address
            scribbled on it – an address in Zurich. She said you
            must have escaped to Zurich.

            (MARGOT *brings her slippers out of her room, then
            returns for a final check of the room.*)

ANNE   Father put that there purposely – just so people would think that very thing.

DUSSEL   And you've been *here* all this time?

MRS FRANK   All this time – ever since July.

(MR FRANK *enters up the stairwell.*)

ANNE   (*to* MR FRANK) It worked, Pim – the address you left. Mr Dussel says that people believe we escaped to Switzerland.

MR FRANK   I'm glad. Let's have a little drink to welcome Mr Dussel. (*He lifts his glass and begins his welcoming toast. All the grown-ups, except* DUSSEL, *rise.* MR FRANK *breaks off as* DUSSEL *bolts his drink. All are amused. He begins again.*) To Mr Dussel. Welcome. We're very honoured to have you with us.

MRS FRANK   To Mr Dussel, welcome.

(*The* VAN DAANS *murmur a welcome. The grown-ups drink.* DUSSEL *is embarrassed as he realizes he has bolted his drink ahead of time.* ANNE *pantomimes drinking a big drink.*)

MRS V. DAAN   Um. That was good.

(MRS FRANK *gives* MARGOT *a sip of her drink, but* MARGOT *does not like it.*)

MR V. DAAN   (*to* DUSSEL) Did Mr Kraler warn you that you won't get much to eat here? You can imagine – three ration

books among the seven of us – and now you make
eight.

(*The sound of the street organ is heard.* MRS VAN DAAN
tugs at her husband's coat-tail. PETER, *humiliated,
rises and moves.*)

DUSSEL   Mr Van Daan, you don't realize what is happening
outside that you should warn me of a thing like that.
You don't realize what's going on. Right here in
Amsterdam every day hundreds of Jews disappear.
They surround a block and search house by house.
Children come back from school to find their parents
gone. Hundreds are being deported – people that you
and I know – the Hallensteins – the Wessels . . .

MRS FRANK   (*in tears*) Oh, no. No!

DUSSEL   They get their call-up notice – come to the Jewish
theatre on such and such a day and hour – bring only
what you can carry in a rucksack. And if you refuse the
call-up notice, then they come and drag you from your
home and ship you off to Mauthausen. The death camp.

MRS FRANK   We didn't know that things had got so much worse.

DUSSEL   Forgive me for speaking so.

ANNE   Do you know the De Waals? Do you know what has
become of them? Their daughter Jopie and I were in
the same class. Jopie's my best friend.

DUSSEL   They are gone.

ANNE   Gone?

DUSSEL   With all the others.

ANNE   Oh, no. Not Jopie! (*She moves up R, in tears.* MARGOT *puts her arm comfortingly around* ANNE.)

MRS V. DAAN   There were some people called Wagner. They lived near us . . .

MR FRANK   (*with a glance at Anne; interrupting*) I think we should put this off until later. We all have many questions we want to ask – but I'm sure that Mr Dussel would like to get settled before supper.

(PETER *gets* DUSSEL'S *things and hands them across the table to* MR FRANK.)

DUSSEL   Thank you. I would. I brought very little with me.

MR FRANK   (*handing the hat and bags to* DUSSEL) I'm sorry we can't give you a room alone. But I hope you won't be too uncomfortable. We've had to make strict rules here – a schedule of hours. We'll tell you after supper. Anne, would you like to take Mr Dussel to his room? (*He moves around the left end of the table, then crosses to* ANNE. DUSSEL *takes a few steps after* MR FRANK *then turns back.*)

ANNE   (*controlling her tears*) If you'll come with me, Mr Dussel. (*She moves to the door of her room.*)

DUSSEL   (*to* MRS VAN DAAN *and shaking her hand*) Forgive me if I haven't really expressed my gratitude to all of you. (*He shakes hands with* MRS FRANK.) This has been such a shock to me. (*He shakes hands with* PETER.) I'd always thought of myself as Dutch. I was born in Holland. My father was born in Holland, and my grandfather. (*He moves to* MARGOT *and shakes hands with her.*) And now – after all these years . . . (*He breaks off.*) If you'll excuse me. (*He shakes hands with* MR VAN DAAN, *then with* MR FRANK *and follows* ANNE *into the room.*)

ANNE   Well, here we are.

(*She closes the door.* DUSSEL *looks around the room. In the centre room* MR FRANK *places a comforting hand on his wife's shoulder.* MARGOT *picks up the cognac.*)

MARGOT   The news sounds pretty bad, doesn't it? It's so different from what Mr Kraler tells us. Mr Kraler says things are improving.

MR V. DAAN   I like it better the way Kraler tells it.

ANNE   You're going to share the room with me.

DUSSEL   I'm a man who's always lived alone. I haven't had to adjust myself to others. I hope you'll bear with me until I learn.

ANNE   Let me help you. (*She takes the bags and places them on the cot.*) Do you always live all alone? Have you no family at all?

DUSSEL   No-one. (*He opens his medicine case and spreads the bottles on the dressing-table.*)

ANNE   How dreadful! You must be terribly lonely.

DUSSEL   I'm used to it.

ANNE I don't think I could ever get used to it. Didn't you even have a pet? A cat, or a dog?

DUSSEL I have an allergy for fur-bearing animals. They give me asthma.

ANNE Oh, dear! Peter has a cat.

DUSSEL Here? (*The very thought makes him choke up*.) He has it here?

ANNE Yes. But we heardly ever see it. He keeps it in his room all the time. I'm sure it will be all right.

DUSSEL Let us hope so. (*He hastily sips some medicine from one of his bottles.*)

ANNE That's Margot's bed, where you're going to sleep. I sleep on the sofa there. (*She indicates the empty books.*) We cleared these off for your things.

(*She climbs up on the window-seat and peers out. DUSSEL sits on the cot to test its softness and is disappointed with it. As ANNE continues, he tests her sofa and finds it more comfortable.*)

The best part about this room — you can look down and see a bit of the street and the canal. There's a houseboat — you can see the end of it — a bargeman lives there with his family. They have a baby and he's just beginning to walk and I'm so afraid he's going to fall into the canal some day. I watch him . . .

DUSSEL Your father spoke of a schedule.

ANNE   Oh, yes.

(*She steps down, then urges him to climb up for a look.* DUSSEL *steps on to the window-seat and peers out of the window.*)

It's mostly about the times we have to be quiet. And times for the WC. (*Without any false shame.*) You can use it now, if you like.

DUSSEL   (*stiffly*) No, thank you.

ANNE   I suppose you think it's awful, my talking about a thing like that. But you don't know how important it can get to be, especially when you're frightened.

(DUSSEL *looks at* ANNE, *appalled at the turn their conversation has taken. As she continues, he takes off his jacket and places it with his bags.*)

About this room, the way Margot and I did – she had it to herself in the afternoons for studying, reading – lessons, you know – and I took the mornings. Would that be all right with you?

DUSSEL   (*removing his tie*) I'm not at my best in the morning.

ANNE   You stay here in the morning, then. I'll take the room in the afternoon.

DUSSEL   Tell me, when you're in here, what happens to me? Where am I spending my time? In there, with all the people?

ANNE   Yes.

DUSSEL   I see, I see.

ANNE   We have supper at half-past six.

DUSSEL   (*moving to the bed and lying on it*) Then, if you don't mind – I like to lie down quietly for ten minutes before eating. I find it helps the digestion.

ANNE   Of course. (*She wonders if she should tell* DUSSEL *he is on the wrong bed, decides not to, moves to him and bends over him.*) I hope I'm not going to be too much of a bother to you. I seem to be able to get everyone's back up.

DUSSEL   (*complacently*) I always get along very well with children. My patients all bring their children to me, because they know I get on well with them. So don't you worry about that. (*He closes his eyes.* ANNE *puts out her hand, wanting to shake hands.*)

ANNE   Thank you. Thank you, Mr Dussel.

(*She taps him on the shoulder.* DUSSEL *jumps, terrified, then takes* ANNE'S *hand.* ANNE *vigorously shakes* DUSSEL'S *hand.* ANNE'S VOICE *comes to us dimly at first and then with increasing power.*)

ANNE'S VOICE   . . . and yesterday I finished Cissy Van Marxvelt's latest book. I think she is a first-class writer. I shall definitely let my children read her. Monday the twenty-first of September, nineteen forty-two. Mr Dussel and I had another battle yesterday. Yes, Mr Dussel. According to him, nothing – I repeat nothing – is right about me, my appearance, my character, my manners. While he was going on at me I thought – sometime I'll give you such a smack that you'll fly right up to the ceiling. Why is it that every grown-up thinks he knows the way to bring up children? Particularly the grown-ups that never had any. I keep wishing Peter was a girl instead of a boy. Then I would have someone to talk to. Margot's a darling, but she takes everything too seriously. To pause for a moment on the subject of Mrs Van Daan.

(*The voice begins to fade.*)

I must tell you that her attempts to flirt with father are getting her nowhere. Pim, thank goodness, won't play.

Scene Four

The same. September 1942. Midnight.

There is darkness except for a little light coming through the skylight, and the faintest trace of a cool glow, making it possible to distinguish the forms of ANNE *in the bed,* DUSSEL *in the cot, and* MR *and* MRS FRANK *asleep on the couch.* MRS FRANK *lies on the seat section,* MR FRANK *on the shelf pulled out from the base. His overcoat is thrown over him.* MARGOT *is asleep up by the shelves with the curtain pulled across the foot of her pallet.* PETER *is asleep. In the attic* MRS VAN DAAN *is asleep in bed.* MR VAN DAAN, *in trousers and undershirt is moving quietly towards the head of the attic stairs. He strikes a match to light his way but extinguishes it at once as he starts down.*

From outside we hear two drunken German soldiers singing 'Lili Marlene'. A girl's high giggle is heard as the trio clumps unsteadily away. As these voices fade away, MR VAN DAAN *strikes another match at the foot of the attic stairs, blows it out, and we hear him open and close the food cupboard under the sink. Outside, we hear running footsteps approach on the cobblestones and pass into the distance. We see* MR VAN DAAN'S *dim figure sneaking back up the attic stairs. After a pause we hear the sound of heavy boots again as they run by and fade away down the street.* MR VAN DAAN *is upstairs again and all is quiet. Suddenly out of the silence and darkness, we hear* ANNE *scream.*

ANNE (*screaming*) No! No! Don't – don't take me. (*She moans, tossing and crying in her sleep. The others wake, terrified.* DUSSEL *sits up in bed, furious.*)

DUSSEL Shush! Anne! Anne, for God's sake, shush!

ANNE (*still in her nightmare*) Save me! Save me! (*She screams and screams.*)

(DUSSEL *gets out of bed, goes to* ANNE *and tries to wake her.*)

DUSSEL For God's sake! Quiet! Quiet! You want someone to hear?

(MRS FRANK *gets out of bed, snatches up her shawl, rushes into to* ANNE, *sits on her bed and takes her in her arms.* MR FRANK *hurriedly gets up and puts on his overcoat.* MARGOT, *terrified, sits up, then rushes over to get the footstool. She drags it so that she can reach the hanging lamp.* PETER *gets up and puts up his blackout curtain. The sound of planes high overhead and ack-ack fire is heard.*)

MRS FRANK Hush, darling, hush. It's all right.

(DUSSEL *blows his nose.*)

There, there – my poor baby – my child. (*To* DUSSEL.)
Will you be kind enough to turn on the light, Mr
Dussel?

(DUSSEL *switches on the pendant.*)

It's nothing, my darling. It was just a dream.

(MARGOT *turns on the pendant.* ANNE *gradually comes
out of her nightmare, still trembling with horror.* MR
FRANK *goes into the room and peers out past the
blackout curtain over the window. He must be sure
that no-one in the street heard the screams.* PETER *slips
into his bath-robe and comes into the centre room.*)

DUSSEL   (*to* MRS FRANK) Something must be done about that
child, Mrs Frank. Yelling like that. Who knows but
there's somebody on the street. She's endangering all
our lives.

(MR VAN DAAN *turns on the attic light and comes down
the stairs.* MARGOT *pulls on her bath-robe, and
switches on the lamp.*)

MRS FRANK   Anne, darling. Little Anne.

DUSSEL   Every night she twists and turns. I don't sleep. I spend
half my night shushing her. And now it's nightmares.

(MRS VAN DAAN *sits up in bed and waits fearfully.* MR
FRANK *moves to* MARGOT *and* PETER *and indicates that
everything is all right.* PETER *takes* MARGOT *back to her
pallet.*)

MRS FRANK   (*to* ANNE) You're here, safe, you see? Nothing has happened. Please, Mr Dussel, go back to bed. She'll be herself in a minute or two. Won't you, Anne?

(DUSSEL *collects his glasses, pillow and a book from the chest.*)

DUSSEL   Thank you, but I'm going to the WC. The one place where there's peace. (*He stalks into the centre room.*)

MR V. DAAN   What is it? What happened?

DUSSEL   A nightmare. She was having a nightmare.

MR V. DAAN   I thought someone was murdering her.

DUSSEL   Unfortunately, no. (*He goes into the WC.*)

(MR VAN DAAN *goes up the attic stairs and explains all to his wife.* MR FRANK *comes into the centre room.*)

MR FRANK   Thank you, Peter. Go back to bed.

(PETER *goes into his room.* MR FRANK *follows him, turns out the lamp and looks out of the window. Then he goes back to the centre room, gets up on the stool and turns off the pendant.* PETER *takes down his blackout curtain, looks for planes for a while, then lies down on his bed in his bath-robe.* MARGOT *sits on her bed.*)

MRS FRANK   Would you like some water?

(ANNE *shakes her head.*)

Was it a very bad dream? Perhaps if you told me . . .?

ANNE   I'd rather not talk about it.

MRS FRANK   Poor darling. Try to sleep, then. I'll sit right here beside
you until you fall asleep. (*She brings the stool from the
dressing-table to* ANNE'S *bed.*)

ANNE   You don't have to.

MRS FRANK   But I'd like to stay with you – very much. Really.

ANNE   I'd rather you didn't.

(MR FRANK *moves to his bed, stands listening to the
planes for a moment, then sits on the end of the bed.*)

MRS FRANK   Good night, then. (*She leans down to kiss* ANNE.)

(ANNE *puts her arm across her face and turns away.*
MRS FRANK *tries not to show her hurt and kisses* ANNE'S
arm instead.)

You'll be all right? There's nothing that you want?

ANNE   Will you please ask father to come.

MRS FRANK   (*after a second*) Of course, Anne dear. (*She hurries
into the centre room, fighting back her tears. She
passes* MR FRANK *and stands below the table.*)

(MR VAN DAAN *turns off the attic light and he and* MRS
VAN DAAN *settle down. The sound of the planes and
ack-ack fire fades.* MRS FRANK *to* MR FRANK.)

She wants you.

MR FRANK   (*sensing her hurt*) Edith, dear.

MRS FRANK   It's all right. I thank God, that at least she will turn to you when she needs comfort. Go to her, Otto. She is still shaking with fear.

(MR FRANK *hesitates.*)

Go to her.

(*She crosses to the bed.* MR FRANK *looks at his wife for a moment, then goes to the shelves, gets a pill from a bottle, collects a cup and goes to the sink for water.* MRS FRANK *sits on the foot of her bed, trying to keep from sobbing aloud.* MARGOT *rises, moves to* MRS FRANK, *sits by her and puts her arms around her.*)

She wants nothing of me. She pulled away when I leaned down to kiss her.

MARGOT   It's a phase – you heard father – most girls go through it – they turn to their fathers at this age – they give all their love to their fathers.

MRS FRANK   You weren't like this. You didn't shut me out.

MARGOT   She'll get over it.

(MR FRANK *goes into the room, pulls the stool aside and places the cup on it.* ANNE *flings her arms around him, clinging to him.* MARGOT *takes the shawl from* MRS FRANK *and smooths the bed.* MRS FRANK *lies down.* MARGOT *sits beside her a moment, comforting her.*)

ANNE   Oh, Pim. I dreamed that they came to get us. The Green Police. They broke down the door and grabbed me and started to drag me out the way they did Jopie.

MR FRANK I want you to take this pill.

ANNE What is it?

MR FRANK Something to quiet you.

(ANNE *takes the pill and drinks some water.*)

Do you want me to read to you for a while?

ANNE No. Just sit with me for a minute.

(MR FRANK *sits on the edge of the bed beside* ANNE, *and puts the cup on the stool.*)

Was I awful? Did I yell terribly loud? Do you think anyone outside could have heard?

(MARGOT *rises and turns out the lamp, then goes back to her bed.*)

MR FRANK No. No. Lie quietly now. Try to sleep.

(ANNE, *still overwrought, lies back.*)

ANNE I'm a terrible coward. I'm so disappointed in myself. I think I've conquered my fear – I think I'm really grown-up – and then something happens – and I run to you like a baby. I love you, Father. I don't love anyone but you.

MR FRANK (*reproachfully*) Anneline!

ANNE It's true. I've been thinking about it for a long time. You're the only one I love.

MR FRANK   It's fine to hear you tell me that you love me. But I'd be much happier if you said you loved your mother as well – she needs your help so much – your love.

ANNE   We have nothing in common. She doesn't understand me. Whenever I try to explain my views on life to her she asks me if I'm constipated.

MR FRANK   You hurt her very much just now. She's crying. She's in there crying.

ANNE   I can't help it. I only told the truth. I didn't want her here. (*With sudden remorse she sits up and clings to* MR FRANK.) Oh, Pim, I was horrible, wasn't I? And the worst of it is, I can stand off and look at myself doing it and know it's cruel and yet I can't stop doing it. What's the matter with me? Tell me. Don't say it's just a phase. Help me.

MR FRANK   There is so little that we parents can do to help our children. We can only try to get a good example – point the way. The rest you must do yourself. You must build your own character.

ANNE   I'm trying. Really I am. (*She lies back more relaxed.*) Every night before I go to sleep I think back over all the things I did that day that were wrong – like putting the wet mop in Mr Dussel's bed – and this thing now with mother. I say to myself, that was wrong. I make up my mind I'm never going to do that again. Never! Of course I may do something worse – but at least I'll never do *that* again. (*The medicine begins to work. She becomes relaxed and drowsy.*) I have a nicer side, Father – a sweeter, nicer side. But I'm scared to show it. I'm afraid that people are going to laugh at me if I'm serious. So the mean Anne comes to the outside, and

the good Anne stays on the inside and I keep on trying
to switch them around and have the good Anne outside
and the bad Anne inside and be what I'd like to be –
and might be – if only – only . . . (*She falls asleep.*)

(MR FRANK *rises quietly, places the cup on the dressing-
table, goes to the door and turns to look at* ANNE *once
more. He turns out the pendant and comes into the
centre room.* MRS FRANK *sits up in bed.* ANNE'S VOICE *comes
to us dimly at first, and then with increasing power.*)

ANNE'S VOICE . . . the air raids are getting worse. They come over day
and night. The noise is terrifying. Pim says it should be
music to our ears. The more planes, the sooner will
come the end of the war. Mrs Van Daan pretends to be
a fatalist. What will be, will be. But when the planes
come over, who is the most frightened? No-one else
but Petronella. Monday, the ninth of November,
nineteen forty-two. Wonderful news. The Allies have
landed in Africa. Pim says that we can look for an early
finish to the war. Just for fun he asked each of us what
was the first thing we wanted to do when we got out of
here. Mrs Van Daan longs to be home with her own
things, her needlepoint chairs, the Bechstein piano her
father gave her – the best that money could buy. Peter
would like to go to a movie. Mr Dussel wants to get
back to his dentist's drill. He's afraid he is losing his
touch. For myself, there are so many things – to ride a
bike again – to laugh till my belly aches – to have new
clothes from the skin out –

(*The voice begins to fade.*)

– to have a hot tub filled to overflowing and wallow in
it for hours – to be back in school with my friends . . .

Scene Five

The same. December 1942. Night.

It is the first night of the Hanukkah celebration in December of that year, 1942. The table has been placed in front of the couch. A tablecloth covers this and is set with a small bowl of sliced apples and walnuts, a small decanter of wine and a pitcher of water. At the end there is a Menorah, improvised by ANNE, *and provided with the Shamos candle and one other candle. The pendant and the table-lamp are on, but the lighting is concentrated on the table area, suggesting a warm candlelight.*

MR FRANK *stands at the end of the table. An armchair is at his place. The 'family' are dressed in their best. The men wear hats.* PETER *wears his cap.* MR FRANK *lights the Shamos, or 'servant candle' on the Menorah before him. He takes it and holds it up as he reads the blessing from a prayer-book.*

MR FRANK   (*reading*) 'Praised by Thou, Oh Lord our God, Ruler of the universe, who has sanctified us with Thy commandments and bidden us kindle the Hanukkah lights. Praised be Thou, Oh Lord our God, Ruler of the universe, who has wrought wondrous deliverances for our fathers in days of old. Praised by Thou, Oh Lord our God, Ruler of the universe, that Thou has given us life and sustenance and brought us to this happy season.' Amen. (*He lights the one candle of the Menorah with the 'servant candle' as he continues.*) 'We kindle this Hanukkah light to celebrate the great and wonderful deeds wrought through the zeal with which God filled the hearts of the heroic Maccabees, two thousand years ago. They fought against indifference, against tyranny and oppression, and they restored our Temple to us. May these lights remind us that we should ever look to God, whence cometh our help.' Amen.

ALL   Amen.

(MR FRANK *hands the prayer-book to* MRS FRANK *and sits as she rises.*)

MRS FRANK   (*reading Psalm one hundred and twenty-one*) 'I lift up mine eyes unto the mountains from whence cometh my help. My help cometh from the Lord who made heaven and earth. He will not suffer thy foot to be moved. He that keepeth thee will not slumber. He that keepeth Israel doth neither slumber nor sleep. The Lord is thy keeper. The Lord is thy shade upon thy right hand. The sun shall not smite thee by day, nor the moon by night. The Lord shall keep thee from evil. He shall keep thy soul. The Lord shall guard thy going out and thy coming in, from this time forth and for evermore.' Amen.

ALL   Amen.

(MRS FRANK *returns the prayer-book to* MR FRANK, *then crosses to the shelves and collects eight plates.* MARGOT *rises, crosses to the shelves and collects eight glasses.*)

DUSSEL   (*rising and handing his hat to* MR FRANK) That was very moving.

ANNE   (*pulling him back*) It isn't over yet.

MRS V. DAAN   Sit down! Sit down!

(MR FRANK *collects* MR VAN DAAN'S *hat and takes it with his own and* DUSSEL'S *and puts them on the mantelpiece, with the prayer-book. He then sits at the head of the table.* PETER *puts his cap in his pocket.* MR VAN DAAN *starts to eat.*)

ANNE   (*to* DUSSEL) There's lots more, songs and presents.

DUSSEL   Presents?

MRS FRANK   Not this year, unfortunately. (*She distributes the plates around the table.*)

MRS V. DAAN   But always on Hanukkah everyone gives presents – everyone.

DUSSEL   Like our St Nicholas' Day.

(*There is a chorus of 'no's' from the others.*)

MRS V. DAAN   No! Not like St Nicholas. What kind of a Jew are you that you don't know Hanukkah?

MRS FRANK   (*to* DUSSEL) I remember particularly the candles. First one, as we have tonight. Then the second night you light two candles, then the next night, three – and so on until you have eight candles burning. When there are eight candles it is truly beautiful.

(MARGOT *places the glasses on the table, then resumes her seat.* DUSSEL *pours the wine.* MRS VAN DAAN *waters hers and* PETER'S *wine.*)

MRS V. DAAN   (*handing a glass to* PETER) And the potato pancakes.

(MRS FRANK *waters the rest of the glasses of wine.*)

MR V. DAAN   Don't talk about them.

MRS V. DAAN   I make the best latkas you ever tasted.

MRS FRANK   Invite us all next year – in your own home.

MR FRANK   Please willing.

MRS V. DAAN   Please willing.

MARGOT   (*rising*) What I remember best is the presents we used to get when we were little – eight days of presents – and each day they got better and better.

MRS FRANK   We are all here, alive. That is present enough.

ANNE   (*excitedly*) No, it isn't. I've got something . . . (*She jumps up and rushes towards her room.*)

MRS FRANK   What is it?

ANNE   Presents. (*She darts into her room and hurriedly puts on a little party hat she has improvised from her lampshade; a paper flower and bits of ribbon cover it. An elastic goes under her chin. She snatches up her school satchel bulging with parcels and comes running back.*)

MRS V. DAAN   (*during this*) Presents!

            (*A toast is led by* MR VAN DAAN.)

ALL   L'chaim, l'chaim!

DUSSEL   (*pointing at* ANNE) Look!

MR V. DAAN   What's she got on her head?

PETER   A lampshade.

ANNE   (*fumbling in the satchel*) Oh, dear. They're every
            which way. (*She pulls out a parcel at random. It is a
            thin book in a manila envelope, with a poem written
            on the outside. She is breathless with excitement.*)
            This is for Margot. (*She moves between* MARGOT *and* MR
            FRANK *and hands the packet to* MARGOT.) Read it out
            loud.

MARGOT   (*reading*)
                    'You have never lost your temper
                    You never will, I fear,
                    You are so good,
                    But if you should,
                    Put all your cross words here.'

            (*She slips the book out of the envelope.*)

MRS FRANK   (*half rising*) What is it?

MARGOT   A new crossword puzzle book. (*To* ANNE.) Where did
            you ever get it?

ANNE   It isn't new. It's one that you've done. But I rubbed it
            all out, and if you wait a little and forget you can do it
            all over again. (*She returns to the satchel.*)

MARGOT   It's wonderful, Anne. Thank you. You'd never know it
            wasn't new.

            (*From outside we hear the sound of a streetcar
            passing.* ANNE *takes a small wrapped bottle half filled
            with liquid from her satchel, crosses and stands
            between her mother and father.*)

ANNE   (*holding out the bottle*) Mrs Van Daan.

MRS V. DAAN (*taking the bottle and unwrapping it*) This is awful –
I haven't anything for anyone – I never thought . . .

MR FRANK This is all Anne's idea.

MRS V. DAAN (*holding up the bottle*) What is it?

ANNE It's hair shampoo. I took all the odds and ends of soap
and mixed them with the last of my toilet water.

MRS V. DAAN Oh, Anneke! (*She takes off the top, sniffs, then lets the
others smell.*)

ANNE (*returning to her satchel*) I wanted to write a poem for
all of them, but I didn't have time. (*She takes out a
shoebox, hides it behind her, and imitates* MR VAN
DAAN'S *walk and voice.*) Yours, Mr Van Daan, is *really*
something – something you want more than anything.
(*She hands the box to* MR VAN DAAN *and waits for him
to open it.*) Look! Cigarettes!

MR V. DAAN (*taking out two dark brown cigarettes; delighted*)
Cigarettes!

ANNE Two of them. Pim found some old pipe tobacco in the
pocket lining of his coat – and we made them – or
rather, Pim did.

MRS V. DAAN Let me see. Well, look at that. Light it, Putti. Light it.

(MR VAN DAAN *hesitates, cigarette in hand, and looks
suspiciously at* ANNE.)

ANNE   (*reassuring him*) It's tobacco, really it is. There's a
little fluff in it, but not much.

(*Everyone watches intently as* MR VAN DAAN *cautiously
lights a cigarette.*)

PETER   It works!

MRS V. DAAN   Look at him!

(*The cigarette flares up. Everyone laughs as* MR VAN
DAAN *coughs and chokes.*)

MR V. DAAN   (*spluttering*) Thank you, Anne. Thank you.

(ANNE *rushes back to her satchel and takes a small
piece of writing paper from it.*)

ANNE   (*crossing to* MRS FRANK *and handing her the paper*) For
Mother, Hanukkah greeting. (*She pulls* MRS FRANK *to her
feet.*)

MRS FRANK   (*reading*)
'Here's an IOU that I promise to pay
Ten hours of doing whatever you say.
Signed, Anne Frank.'

(*Touched, she takes* ANNE *in her arms and holds her
close.*)

DUSSEL   (*to* ANNE) Ten hours of doing what you're told?
Anything you're told?

ANNE   That's right. (*She returns to her satchel.*)

DUSSEL   (*after thinking it over for a second*) You wouldn't
want to sell that, Mrs Frank?

MRS FRANK   Never! This is the most precious gift I've ever had. (*She
sits and shows the piece of paper to the others.* ANNE
pulls out a scarf.)

ANNE   For Pim.

MR FRANK   Anneke – I wasn't supposed to have a present. (*He
takes the scarf, unfolds it, shows it to the others, then
puts it on and tucks it inside his jacket.*)

ANNE   It's a muffler – to put around your neck. I made it
myself out of odds and ends – I knitted it in the dark
each night, after I'd gone to bed. (*Ruefully.*) I'm afraid
it looks better in the dark. (*She gets* PETER'S *and*
MOUSCHI'S *presents from her satchel.*)

MR FRANK   It's fine. It fits me perfectly. Thank you, Anneke.

ANNE   (*going to* PETER *and handing him a ball of paper with a
ribbon and little bells attached to it*) That's for Mouschi.

PETER   (*rising and bowing*) On behalf of Mouschi, I thank you.

ANNE   (*handing* PETER *a small package; hesitantly*) And –
this is yours – from Mrs Quack Quack.

(PETER *holds the little case gingerly in his hands.*)

Well – open it. Aren't you going to open it?

PETER   I'm scared to. I know something's going to jump out
and hit me.

ANNE   No. It's nothing like that, really.

          (PETER *opens the case.*)

MRS V. DAAN   What is it, Peter? Go on. Show it.

ANNE   (*excitedly*) It's a safety razor.

DUSSEL   A what?

ANNE   A razor.

MRS V. DAAN   You didn't make that out of odds and ends.

ANNE   (*to* PETER) Miep got it for me. It's not new. It's
           secondhand. But you really do need a razor, now.

DUSSEL   For what?

ANNE   (*pointing to* PETER) Look on his upper lip – you can
           see the beginning of a moustache.

DUSSEL   He wants to get rid of that? Put a little milk on it and
           let the cat lick it off.

PETER   (*rising and crossing to his room*) Think you're funny,
           don't you?

DUSSEL   Look! He can't wait. He's going to try it.

PETER   I'm going in to give Mouschi his present. (*He goes into
           his room, slams the door behind him, sits on the
           window-seat, rolls up a towel and tucks it into his
           jacket.*)

MR V. DAAN   (*disgustedly*) Mouschi, Mouschi, Mouschi.

(*In the distance we hear a dog persistently barking.* ANNE *brings a gift to* DUSSEL.)

ANNE   And last but never least, my room-mate, Mr Dussel.

DUSSEL   For me? You have something for me?

(ANNE *hands a tiny box to* DUSSEL, *who beams and opens it*.)

ANNE   I made them myself.

DUSSEL   (*puzzled*) Capsules! Two capsules.

ANNE   (*excitedly*) They're ear-plugs.

DUSSEL   Ear-plugs?

ANNE   To put in your ears so you won't hear me when I thrash around at night. I saw them advertised in a magazine. They're not real ones – I made them out of cotton and candle wax. Try them – see if they don't work – see if you can hear me talk.

DUSSEL   (*putting a capsule in his right ear*) Wait now until I get them in – (*He puts a capsule in the left ear.*) so.

ANNE   Are you ready?

DUSSEL   Huh?

ANNE   (*louder*) Are you ready?

DUSSEL   (*rising with an agonized look on his face*) Good God! They've gone inside. (*He thumps his head and tries frantically to get out the ear plugs.*)

(*Everyone laughs except* ANNE, *who is chagrined at the turn of events.*)

I can't get them out. (*Finally he gets them out.*) Thank you, Anne. Thank you. (*He pockets the plugs.*)

MR V. DAAN		A real Hanukkah!
MRS V. DAAN	(*together*)	Wasn't it cute of her?
MRS FRANK		I don't know when she did it.
MARGOT		I love my present.

ANNE   And now let's have the song, Father – please. Have you heard the Hanukkah song, Mr Dussel? The song is the whole thing. (*She sings enthusiastically.*)

> 'Oh, Hanukkah, Oh Hanukkah.
> A sweet celebration . . .'

MR FRANK   (*quietening* ANNE) I'm afraid, Anne, we shouldn't sing that song tonight. (*To* DUSSEL.) It's a song of jubilation, of rejoicing. One is apt to become too enthusiastic.

ANNE   Oh, please, please. Let's sing the song. I promise not to shout.

(PETER *rises and comes into the centre room, ostentatiously holding a bulge in his coat as if he were holding his cat, and dangling Mouschi's present before it.*)

MR FRANK   Very well. But quietly now – I'll keep an eye on you, and when . . .

(DUSSEL *points at* PETER *and begins to wheeze and cough.*)

DUSSEL You – you. How many times . . . I told you . . . Out! Out!

(MR VAN DAAN *rises, brushes past his wife and strides to* PETER.)

MR V. DAAN What's the matter with you? Haven't you any sense? Get that cat out of here.

PETER (*innocently*) Cat?

MR V. DAAN You heard me. Get it out of here.

PETER I have no cat. (*Delighted with his joke, he pulls the towel from his coat and holds it high for all to see. The group at the table laugh, enjoying the joke.*)

DUSSEL (*still wheezing*) It doesn't need to be the cat – his clothes are enough – (*He coughs unconvincingly to prove his point.*) when he comes out of that room . . .

MR V. DAAN Don't worry. You won't be bothered any more. We're getting rid of it.

DUSSEL At last you listen to me. (*He goes into his room.*)

MR V. DAAN (*calling after him*) I'm not doing it for you. That's all in your mind – all of it.

(DUSSEL *takes a swallow of his medicine then sits on his bed to recover.*)

I'm doing it because I'm sick of seeing that cat eat all our food.

PETER   That's not true. I only give him bones – scraps . . .

MR V. DAAN   Don't tell me! He gets fatter every day. Damn cat looks better than any of us. Out he goes tonight.

PETER   No! No!

ANNE   Mr Van Daan, you can't do that. That's Peter's cat. Peter loves that cat.

MRS FRANK   Anne.

PETER   If he goes, I go.

MR V. DAAN   Go! Go!

MRS V. DAAN   You're not going and the cat's not going. Now, please – this is Hanukkah – Hanukkah – this is the time to celebrate – what's the matter with all of you? Come on, Anne. Let's have the song.

ANNE

'Oh, Hanukkah, Oh, Hanukkah.
The sweet celebration . . .'

MR FRANK   I think we should first blow out the candle –

(MARGOT *makes a little sound of protest.*)

– then we'll have something for tomorrow night.

MARGOT   But, Father, you're supposed to let them burn themselves out.

MR FRANK   I'm sure that God understands shortages. (*He prays.*)
'Praised be Thou, Oh Lord our God, who hast sustained
us and permitted us to celebrate this joyous festival.'
Amen. (*He leans forward to blow out the candles.*)

(*There is a sudden crash of something falling below.
The dogs starts to bark again. They all freeze in
horror, motionless, straining to hear. For a few
seconds there is complete silence, then* MRS FRANK
snatches off her shoes, rises, and switches off the lamp.
MR FRANK *hurries to the head of the stair-well.* MR VAN
DAAN *rises and follows him. All take off their shoes.* MR
FRANK *signals to* PETER *to turn off the pendant.* PETER
*cannot reach the chain so he pulls a chair to a
position under the lamp, and stands on it. Just as he
is touching the lamp he loses his balance. The chair
goes out from under him. He falls. The iron shade
crashes to the floor. The light of the pendant goes out.
There is a sound of feet below, running down the
stairs.* PETER *picks himself up immediately.*)

MR V. DAAN   (*under his breath*) God Almighty!

(DUSSEL *rises, and moves towards* PETER, *gesturing for
silence.* MARGOT *rises.* ANNE *rises.* MR VAN DAAN *listens
intently. The footsteps die away. The following lines
are whispered.*)

Do you hear anything?

(MR FRANK *listens carefully for another moment.*)

MR FRANK   No. I think they've gone.

MRS V. DAAN   (*with a trace of hysteria in her voice*) It's the Green
Police. They've found us.

MR FRANK   If they had, they wouldn't have left. They'd be up here by now.

MRS V. DAAN   I know it's the Green Police. They've gone to get help. That's all. They'll be back.

MR V. DAAN   Or it may have been the Gestapo, looking for papers.

MR FRANK   Or a thief, looking for money.

MRS V. DAAN   We've got to do something. Quick! Quick! Before they come back.

MR V. DAAN   There isn't anything to do. Just wait.

(MR FRANK *holds up his hand for them to be quiet, and listens intently. There is complete silence as they all strain to hear any sound from below. Suddenly* ANNE *begins to sway. With a low cry she falls to the floor in a faint.* MRS FRANK *goes quickly to* ANNE *and sits on the floor, lifting* ANNE'S *head on to her lap.*)

MRS FRANK   Get some water, please. Get some water.

(MARGOT *moves towards the sink.*)

MR V. DAAN   (*grabbing* MARGOT) No. No. No-one's going to run water.

MR FRANK   If they've found us, they've found us. Get the water.

(MARGOT *continues to the sink.* MR FRANK *moves to the shelves and picks up a torch.*)

I'm going down.

(MARGOT *rushes to* MR FRANK *and clings to him as he moves to the stairwell.* ANNE *struggles back to consciousness.*)

MARGOT   No, Father, No. There may be someone there, waiting – it may be a trap.

MR FRANK   This is Saturday. There is no way for us to know what has happened until Miep or Mr Kraler come on Monday morning. We cannot live with this uncertainty.

MARGOT   Don't go, Father.

MRS FRANK   Hush, darling, hush.

(MR FRANK *shakes* MARGOT *off and exits quietly down the stairwell.*)

Margot. Stay close to me.

(MARGOT *goes to* MRS FRANK.)

MR V. DAAN   Shush! Shush!

(MARGOT *remembers the water, gets some from the sink, then kneels and gives* ANNE *a sip.*)

MRS V. DAAN   (*becoming hysterical*) Putti, where's our money? Get our money. I hear you can buy the Green Police off, so much a head. Go upstairs, quick. Get the money.

MR V. DAAN   Keep still.

MRS V. DAAN   (*pleading*) Do you want to be dragged off to a concentration camp? Are you going to stand there and wait for them to come up and get you? (*She sinks to her knees in front of her husband as her hysteria mounts.*) Do something, I tell you.

MR V. DAAN   Will you keep still! (*He shoves her aside and crosses quietly and quickly to the stair-well and listens.* MRS VAN DAAN *falls sobbing against the couch.*)

(PETER *hurries to her and helps her to sit on the couch. There is a second of silence, then* ANNE *can stand it no longer.*)

ANNE   Someone go after father. Make father come back.

(MRS FRANK *covers* ANNE'S *mouth to muffle her voice.*)

PETER   (*hurrying to the stairwell*) I'll go.

MR V. DAAN   (*pushing* PETER *roughly*) Haven't you done enough?

(PETER *grabs a chair as if to hit* MR VAN DAAN *with it, then puts it down and buries his face in his hands.*)

ANNE   Please, please, Mr Van Daan. Get father.

MR V. DAAN   Quiet! Quiet!

(ANNE *is shocked into silence.* MRS FRANK *pulls* ANNE *closer, holding her protectively in her arms.*)

MRS FRANK   (*praying softly*) 'I lift up mine eyes unto the mountains, from whence cometh my help. My help cometh from the Lord who made heaven and earth. He will not suffer thy foot to be moved. He that keepeth thee will not slumber . . .' (*She breaks off as she hears someone coming.*)

(*They all watch the stairwell tensely.* MR FRANK *enters up the stair-well.* ANNE *rises, rushes to* MR FRANK *and holds him tightly.* MRS FRANK *and* MARGOT *rise.*)

MR FRANK   It was a thief. That noise must have scared him away.

MRS V. DAAN   Thank God!

MR FRANK   He took the cash box. And the radio. He ran away in such a hurry that he didn't stop to shut the street door. It was swinging wide open.

(*A breath of relief sweeps over the others.*)

I think it'd be good to have some light.

MARGOT   Are you sure it's all right?

MR FRANK   The danger has passed.

(MARGOT *goes to the table-lamp and switches it on.*)

Don't be so terrified, Anne. We're safe.

DUSSEL   Who says the danger has passed? Don't you realize we are in greater danger than ever?

MR FRANK   Mr Dussel, will you be still.

DUSSEL (*pointing to* PETER) Thanks to this clumsy fool, there's someone now who knows we're up here. Someone now knows we're up here, hiding.

MRS V. DAAN Someone knows we're here, yes. But who is the someone? A thief. You think a thief is going to go to the Green Police and say – I was robbing a place the other night and I heard a noise up over my head? You think a thief is going to do that?

DUSSEL Yes. I think he will.

MRS V. DAAN (*hysterically*) You're crazy. (*She stumbles back to her seat at the table.*)

(PETER *follows protectively, pushes* DUSSEL *aside, then sits on his stool and comforts his mother.*)

DUSSEL I think some day he'll be caught and then he'll make a bargain with the Green Police – if they'll let him off, he'll tell them where some Jews are hiding. (*He goes into his room and sinks down on to his bed.*)

MR V. DAAN He's right.

ANNE (*terrified*) Father, let's get out of here. We can't stay here now. Let's go.

MR V. DAAN Go! Where?

MRS FRANK (*sinking into her place at the table; in despair*) Yes. Where?

(MR FRANK *rises quickly and surveys the 'family' as they slump in their places. He knows he must restore their courage.*)

MR FRANK   Have we lost all faith? All courage? A moment ago we
           thought that they'd come for us. We were sure it was
           the end. But it wasn't the end. We're alive, safe. (*He
           prays.*) We thank Thee, Oh Lord our God, that in Thy
           infinite mercy Thou hast seen fit to spare us. (*He blows
           out the candles, then turns to* ANNE.) Come on, Anne.
           The song. The song.

           (ANNE *starts falteringly to sing. Her voice is hardly
           audible at first.*)

ANNE   (*singing*)
                'Oh, Hanukkah. Oh, Hanukkah.
                The sweet celebration.'

           (*As she goes on singing, one by one the others join in.
           There is no unity, no rhythm at first.* MRS VAN DAAN *sobs
           as she sings.* DUSSEL *rises and comes out of his room.*
           MARGOT *draws him into the group. As they sing, 'Many
           are the reasons for good cheer', their courage and
           faith are beginning to return.*)

ALL   (*singing*)
                'Around the feast we gather
                In complete jubilation.
                Happiest of seasons
                Now is here.
                Many are the reasons for good cheer.
                Together
                We'll weather
                Whatever tomorrow may bring.'

           (*They sing on with growing courage.*)

                'So hear us rejoicing
                And merrily voicing

The Hanukkah song that we sing.
Hoy!
Hear us rejoicing
And merrily voicing
The Hanukkah song that we sing.'

CURTAIN

ACT TWO

Scene One

The same, January 1944. Late afternoon.

ANNE'S VOICE *is heard reading from the diary.*

ANNE'S VOICE Saturday, the first of January, nineteen forty-four.
Another new year has begun and we find ourselves still
in our hiding place. We have been here now for one
year, five months, and twenty-five days. It seems that
our life is at a standstill.

(*It is late afternoon of a cold winter day. In the centre
room* MRS FRANK, *in sweater, apron and fingerless
gloves, takes down the laundry and exits with it
above the kitchen area.* MR FRANK, *also in a sweater,
sits reading in his armchair at the extreme down L
corner of the room. His back is three-quarters to the
audience.* MARGOT *lies on the couch with a blanket
over her and the many-coloured knitted scarf around
her throat.* PETER *sits under the skylight, reading. He is
wearing his suit jacket with the collar turned up and
a knitted cap. The* VAN DAANS *are in the attic room.* MRS
VAN DAAN *is wearing* PETER'S *raincoat.* MR VAN DAAN *is in
sweater and gloves.* DUSSEL *lies asleep on his bed.*)

We are all a little thinner. The Van Daans' 'discussions'
are as violent as ever. Mother still does not understand
me. But then I don't understand her, either. There is
one great change, however. A change in myself. I read
somewhere that girls of my age don't feel quite certain
of themselves. That they become quiet within and

begin to think of the miracle that is taking place in their bodies. I think that what is happening to me is so wonderful – not only what can be seen, but what is taking place inside. Each time it has happened I have a feeling that I have a – (ANNE'S VOICE *hesitates a second.*) – sweet secret.

(*We hear the carillon chimes begin a hymn.* ANNE'S VOICE *fades slowly.*)

And in spite of my pain, I long for the time when I shall feel that secret within me again.

(*There is a pause. The pause is broken by* MIEP'S *signal on the door buzzer. Everyone is momentarily startled.* MRS FRANK *hurries anxiously back into the centre room.*)

MR FRANK   It's Miep. (*He goes quickly down the stairs to unbolt the door.*)

MRS FRANK   Wake up, everyone. Miep is here.

(MIEP *enters up the stairs. She carries a small bunch of flowers and a bag of food.* KRALER *follows* MIEP *on. He carries a small package and a bunch of flowers. They are both bundled up against the cold.*)

Miep – *and* Mr Kraler – what a delightful surprise.

(MIEP, *after giving a warm greeting and the bag of food to* MRS FRANK, *crosses to* ANNE *and they affectionately embrace.* PETER *rises and comes into the centre room.*)

KRALER (*giving the package to* MRS FRANK) We came to bring
you New Year's greetings.

MRS FRANK You shouldn't – you should have at least one day to
yourselves.

(KRALER *greets* PETER.)

ANNE Don't say that, it's so wonderful to see them. (*She sniffs
at* MIEP'S *coat.*) I can smell the wind and the cold on
your clothes.

MIEP (*giving* ANNE *the flowers*) There you are.

(*She crosses to* MARGOT *and feels her forehead.*)

How are you, Margot? Feeling any better?

MARGOT I'm all right.

ANNE We filled her full of every kind of pill so she won't
cough and make a noise. (*She puts the diary into the
window-seat, takes a glass of water from the chest of
drawers, puts her flowers in it, then puts them on the
dressing-table. The carillon hymn finishes.*)

(*The* VAN DAANS *come down the attic stairs. Outside
there is the sound of a band playing.*)

MRS V. DAAN Well, hello, Miep. Mr Kraler.

KRALER (*moving to* MRS VAN DAAN *and giving her the flowers*)
With my hope for peace in the New Year.

(MIEP *acknowledges the* VAN DAANS' *greetings.*)

PETER Miep, have you seen Mouschi? Have you seen him
anywhere around?

MIEP   I'm sorry, Peter. I asked everyone in the
neighbourhood had they seen a grey cat. But they said
'no'.

(MRS VAN DAAN *places her flowers in the sink.* MR FRANK
*comes up the stairs. He carries two books and a small
cake on a plate, inscribed 'Peace in 1944'.*)

MR FRANK   Look what Miep's brought for us. (*He places the cake
on the table.*)

MRS FRANK   A cake!

MR V. DAAN   A cake! I'll get some plates.

(DUSSEL *hastily puts on a coat, rises and comes into
the centre room.*)

MRS FRANK   Thank you, Miepia. You shouldn't have done it. You
must have used all of your sugar ration for weeks. (*She
picks up the cake and hands it to* MRS VAN DAAN.) It's
beautiful, isn't it?

MRS V. DAAN   (*to* MIEP) It's been ages since I even saw a cake. Not
since you brought us one last year.

(MRS FRANK *gets the teapot from the draining-board,
goes to the stove, pours hot water into the teapot, then
brings it to the table.*)

Remember? Don't you remember, you gave us one on
New Year's Day? Just this time last year? I'll never
forget it because you had 'Peace in nineteen forty-
three' on it. (*She looks at the cake and reads.*) 'Peace
in nineteen forty-four.'

MIEP Well, it has to come sometime, you know. (*She looks across at* DUSSEL) Hello, Mr Dussel. (*She crosses quickly to Dussel, shakes hands with him.*)

(MRS FRANK *brings four cups from the draining-board and puts them on the table.*)

KRALER (*to* DUSSEL) How are you? (*He shakes hands with* DUSSEL.)

(MR VAN DAAN *brings plates, forks and a knife from the shelves and puts them on the table.*)

MR V. DAAN (*to his wife*) Here's the knife, liefje. Now, how many of us are there?

MIEP } (*together*) None for me, thank you.
KRALER   No, thanks.

MR FRANK Oh, please. You must.

MIEP I couldn't.

MR V. DAAN Good!

(MRS FRANK *gets four more cups from the draining-board and puts them on the table.* MRS VAN DAAN *crosses to the table, places the cake on it and sits.*)

That leaves one – two – three – seven of us.

DUSSEL (*pointing to himself*) Eight! Eight! It's the same number as it always is.

MR V. DAAN I left Margot out. I take it for granted Margot won't eat any.

ANNE   Why wouldn't she?

MRS FRANK   (*pouring tea*) I think it won't harm her.

MR V. DAAN   All right. All right. I just didn't want her to start coughing again, that's all.

DUSSEL   And please, Mrs Frank should cut the cake.

MR V. DAAN   ⎫ (*together*)   What's the difference?
MRS V. DAAN   ⎭   It's not Mrs Frank's cake, is it, Miep? It's for all of us.

DUSSEL   Mrs Frank divides things better.

MRS V. DAAN   ⎫ (*together*)   What are you trying to say?
MR V. DAAN   ⎭   Oh, come on. Stop wasting time.

MRS V. DAAN   (*confronting* DUSSEL) Don't I always give everybody exactly the same? Don't I?

MR V. DAAN   Forget it, Kerli.

MRS V. DAAN   No. I want an answer. (*To* DUSSEL.) Don't I?

DUSSEL   Yes. Yes. Everybody gets exactly the same –

(MRS VAN DAAN, *satisfied, turns away to the cake.*)

– except Mr Van Daan always gets a little bit more.

(*The* VAN DAANS *whirl and come back at* DUSSEL, MR VAN DAAN *holding the knife.* DUSSEL *retreats before their onslaught to the WC steps.* MRS FRANK *returns to the table, picks up a cup of tea and hands it to* MIEP.)

MR V. DAAN   That's a lie. She always cuts the same.

MR FRANK   Please, please. (*He moves to* MIEP. *Apologetically.*) You see what a little sugar cake does to us? It goes right to our heads.

MR V. DAAN   (*handing the knife to* MRS FRANK) Here you are, Mrs Frank.

(MR FRANK *crosses and stands below the table, to help* MRS FRANK.)

MRS FRANK   Thank you. (*To* MIEP.) Are you sure you won't have some? (*She cuts the cake.*)

MIEP   No, really. I have to go in a minute. (*She drinks her tea.*)

PETER   (*moving to* MIEP) Maybe Mouschi went back to our house – they say that cats . . . Do you ever get over there? I mean – do you suppose you could . . .?

(MR VAN DAAN *snatches the first piece of cake.* MRS VAN DAAN *gets the second piece on a plate and takes it to the stove, where she stands and eats.*)

MIEP   I'll try, Peter. The first minute I get I'll try. But I'm afraid, with him gone a week . . .

DUSSEL   Make up your mind, already someone has had a nice big dinner from that cat.

(PETER *is furous and inarticulate. He starts towards*
DUSSEL *as if to hit him.* MR FRANK *restrains* PETER. MRS
FRANK *speaks quickly to* MIEP *to ease the situation.*)

MRS FRANK   This is delicious, Miep. (*She hands cake to* DUSSEL.)

MRS V. DAAN   Delicious!

(MR VAN DAAN *sits and wolfs his cake.* MRS FRANK *hands
cake to* MR FRANK *and* ANNE.)

MR V. DAAN   Dirk's in luck to get a girl who can bake like this.

MIEP   (*putting her empty cup on the table*) I have to run.
Dirk's taking me to a party tonight.

(MRS FRANK *takes cake to* MARGOT, *then puts the
remaining pieces on plates.*)

ANNE   (*to* MIEP) How heavenly! Remember now what
everyone is wearing, and what you have to eat and
everything, so you can tell us tomorrow.

MIEP   I'll give you a full report. Good-bye, everyone. (*She
turns to the stairwell.*)

MR V. DAAN   (*to* MIEP) Just a minute. There's something I'd like you
to do for me. (*He hurries up the stairs to the attic
room.*)

MRS V. DAAN   Putti, where are you going? What do you want? Putti,
what are you going to do? (*She rushes up the stairs
after him.*)

MIEP   (*to* PETER) What's wrong?

PETER   (*his sympathy with his mother*) Father says he's going to sell her fur coat. She's crazy about that old fur coat.

DUSSEL Is it possible? Is it possible that anyone is so silly as to worry about a fur coat in times like this?

(PETER *advances on* DUSSEL *but is restrained by* MR FRANK.)

PETER   (*to* DUSSEL) It's none of your darn business – and if you say one more thing – I'll – I'll take you and I'll . . . I mean it – I'll . . .

(*Suddenly there is a piercing scream from* MRS VAN DAAN *in the attic room. She grabs at the fur coat as* MR VAN DAAN *passes her to go downstairs with it.*)

MRS V. DAAN   No! No! No! Don't you dare take that. You hear? It's mine.

(PETER, *embarrassed and miserable, goes to the stairs but can do nothing.*)

My father gave me that. You didn't give it to me. You have no right. Let go of it – you hear?

(MR VAN DAAN *pulls the coat from her hands and hurries down the attic stairs. As he comes into the centre room the others look away, embarrassed for him.* MRS VAN DAAN, *sobbing, sinks to the attic floor.*)

MR V. DAAN   (*to* KRALER) Just a little – discussion over the advisability of selling this coat. As I have often reminded Mrs Van Daan, it's very selfish of her to keep it when people outside are in such desperate need of clothing. (*He gives the coat to* MIEP.) So if you will please to sell it for us? It should fetch a good price.

(MIEP *turns to go. With an afterthought.*)

And, by the way, will you get me cigarettes? I don't care what kind they are – get all you can.

MIEP   It's terribly difficult to get them, Mr Van Daan. But I'll try. Good-bye.

MRS FRANK   Good-bye.

MR FRANK   Good-bye, Miep.

(MIEP *exits down the stairs.* MR FRANK *follows her down the steps and bolts the door after her.* MRS FRANK *rises and gives* KRALER *a cup of tea.*)

MRS FRANK   Are you sure you won't have some cake, Mr Kraler?

KRALER   I'd better not.

MR V. DAAN   You're still feeling badly? What does the doctor say?

KRALER   I haven't been to him.

MRS FRANK   Now, Mr Kraler . . .

KRALER   Oh, I tried. But you can't get near a doctor these days – they're so busy. After weeks I finally managed to get

one on the telephone. I told him I'd like an
appointment – I wasn't feeling very well. You know
what he answers – over the telephone – 'Stick out your
tongue.' (*They laugh. He turns to* MR FRANK.) I have
some contracts here – I wonder if you'd look over
them with me.

MR FRANK   (*holding out his hand*) Of course.

KRALER   (*rising*) If we could go downstairs . . .

(MR FRANK *rises and goes down the stairs. He turns to
the others.*)

Will you forgive us? I won't keep him a minute. (*He
moves to the stairs.*)

MARGOT   (*with sudden foreboding*) What's happened?
Something's happened. Hasn't it, Mr Kraler?

(KRALER *stops and turns, moves below the table and
tries to reassure* MARGOT *with a pretence of
casualness.*)

KRALER   No, really. I want your father's advice . . .

MARGOT   Something's gone wrong. I know it.

MR FRANK   (*coming back; to* KRALER) If it's something that
concerns us here, it's better that we all hear it.

KRALER   (*turning to* MR FRANK; *quietly*) But – the children . . .?

MR FRANK   What they'd imagine would be worse than any reality.

(KRALER *is reluctant, but begins his story. They all listen with intense apprehension and move slowly to sit.*)

KRALER   It's a man in the storeroom. I don't know whether or not you remember him – Carl, about fifty, heavy-set, near-sighted. He came with us just before you left.

MR FRANK   He was from Utrecht?

KRALER   That's the man. A couple of weeks ago, when I was in the storeroom, he closed the door and asked me: 'How's Mr Frank? What do you hear from Mr Frank?' I told him I only knew there was a rumour that you were in Switzerland. He said he'd heard that rumour, too, but he thought I might know something more. I didn't pay any attention to it – but then a thing happened yesterday. He'd brought some invoices to the office for me to sign. As I was going through them, I looked up. He was standing staring at the bookcase – (*He indicates the door at the foot of the stairwell.*) the bookcase that hides your door. He said he thought he remembered a door there – wasn't there a door there that used to go up to the loft? Then he told me he wanted more money. Twenty guilders more a week.

(MRS VAN DAAN *rises, comes slowly down the attic steps and sits on the bottom step, listening.*)

MR V. DAAN   (*bursting out*) Blackmail!

MR FRANK   (*calmly*) Twenty guilders? Very modest blackmail.

MR V. DAAN   That's just the beginning.

DUSSEL   You know what I think? He was the thief who was down there that night. That's how he knows we're here.

MR FRANK   (*to* KRALER) How was it left? What did you tell him?

KRALER   I said I had to think about it. What shall I do? Pay him the money – take a chance on firing him – or what? I don't know.

DUSSEL   For God's sake don't fire him. Pay him what he asks – keep him here where you can have your eye on him.

MR FRANK   Is it so much that he's asking? What are they paying nowadays?

KRALER   He could get it in a war plant. But this isn't a war plant. (*He turns to reassure the others.*) Mind you, I don't know if he really knows – or if he doesn't know.

MR FRANK   Offer him half. Then we'll soon find out if it's blackmail or not.

DUSSEL   And if it is? We've got to pay it, haven't we? Anything he asks we've got to pay.

MR FRANK   (*patiently and calmly*) Let's decide that when the time comes.

KRALER   (*again trying to reassure them*) This may be all my imagination. You get to a point, these days, where you suspect everyone and everything. Again and again – on some simple look or word, I've found myself . . .

(*The telephone rings in the office below.*)

MRS V. DAAN   There's the telephone. What does that mean, the telephone ringing on a holiday?

KRALER   That's my wife. I told her I had to go over some papers in my office – to call me there when she got out of church. (*He rises.*) I'll offer him half, then. (*He shakes hands with* MR FRANK.) Good-bye – we'll hope for the best.

(MR FRANK *rises. The others half-heartedly call their 'good-byes'.* KRALER *exits down the stairwell.* MR FRANK *follows him down and bolts the door below.* MRS FARNK *rises to see* KRALER *out, then sits dispiritedly in the chair above the stairwell. After a moment* MR VAN DAAN *slaps his knee in a gesture of resignation, then rises and takes his and* MARGOT'S *china to the sink.* MRS VAN DAAN *goes into the WC.*)

DUSSEL   (*to* MR VAN DAAN) You can thank your son for this – (*He points to the pendant.*) smashing the light. I tell you, it's just a question of time, now. (*He stands looking out of the window.*)

(MR FRANK *comes up the stairwell.*)

MARGOT   Sometimes I wish the end would come – whatever it is.

MRS FRANK   (*rising; shocked*) Margot!

(ANNE *rises, goes to* MARGOT, *sits beside her on the couch and puts her arms around her.*)

MARGOT   Then at least we'd know where we were.

MRS FRANK You should be ashamed of yourself. Talking that way.
Think how lucky we are. Think of the thousands dying
in the war, every day. Think of the people in
concentration camps.

ANNE What's the good of that? What's the good of thinking of
misery when you're already miserable? That's stupid!

MRS FRANK Anne!

ANNE We're young, Margot and Peter and I. (*She rises.*) You
grown-ups have had your chance. But look at us. If we
begin thinking of all the horrors in the world, we're
lost. We're trying to hold on to some kind of ideals –
when everything – ideals, hopes – everything, are
being destroyed.

MRS FRANK Now, Anne . . .

ANNE It isn't our fault that the world is in such a mess. We
weren't around when all this started.

MRS FRANK Anne!

ANNE So don't try to take it out on us. (*She rushes into her
room, slams the door after her, picks up a brush from
the chest and hurls it to the floor. Then she sits on her
bed, trying to control her anger.*)

MR V. DAAN She talks as if we started the war. Did we start the war?

(*He sees* ANNE'S *cake on the table and reaches out to
take it.* PETER *anticipates* MR VAN DAAN *and picks up the
plate.*)

PETER   She left her cake.

(MR VAN DAAN *looks after* PETER, *then turns and goes up the attic stairs.* MR FRANK *gives* MRS FRANK *her cake, and she sits, eating without relish.* MR FRANK *then takes a piece of cake to* MARGOT *and sits quietly on the couch above her, as she slowly eats.* PETER *goes into* ANNE'S *room.* ANNE *sits up quickly, trying to hide the signs of her tears.* PETER *holds out the cake.*)

You left this.

ANNE   (*dully*) Thanks.

(PETER *places the cake on the window-seat, then moves to the door, changes his mind, closes the door and turns to* ANNE.)

PETER   I thought you were fine, just now. You know just how to talk to them. You know just how to say it. I'm no good – I never can think – especially when I'm mad. That Dussel – when he said that about Mouschi – someone eating him – all I could think is – I wanted to hit him. I wanted to give him such a – a – that he'd . . . That's what I used to do when there was an argument at school – that's the way I – but here – and an old man like that – it wouldn't be so good.

ANNE   You're making a big mistake about me. I do it all wrong. I say too much. I go too far. I hurt people's feelings.

PETER   I think you're just fine – what I want to say – if it wasn't for you around here, I don't know. What I mean is . . .

(DUSSEL *enters the room.* ANNE *and* PETER *turn to look at him.* DUSSEL *pauses a second, staring back, then moves towards his bed.* PETER *advances towards him, slowly and menacingly.* DUSSEL *retreats, backing out of the door. He looks back forlornly as* PETER *firmly closes the door on him and returns to* ANNE.)

ANNE   Do you mean it, Peter? Do you really mean it?

PETER   I said it, didn't I?

ANNE   Thank you, Peter.

PETER   (*looking at the pictures on the wall*) You've got quite a collection.

ANNE   Would you like some in your room? I could give you some. Heaven knows you spend enough time in there – doing Heaven knows what.

PETER   It's easier. A fight starts, or an argument – I duck in there.

ANNE   You're lucky, having a room to go to. His lordship is always here – I hardly ever get a minute alone. When they start in on me, I can't duck away. I have to stand there and take it.

PETER   You gave some of it back just now.

ANNE   I get so mad. They've formed their opinions – about everything – but we – we're still trying to find out. We have problems here that no other people our age have ever had. And just as you think you've solved them, something comes along and bang – you have to start all over again.

PETER   At least you've got someone you can talk to.

ANNE   Not really. Mother – I never discuss anything serious with her. She doesn't understand. Father's all right. We can talk about everything – everything but one thing. Mother. He simply won't talk about her. I don't think you can be really intimate with anyone if he holds something back, do you?

PETER   I think your father's fine.

ANNE   Oh, he is, Peter. He is. He's the only one who's ever given me the feeling that I have any sense. But, anyway, nothing can take the place of school and friends of your own age – or near your age – can it?

PETER   I suppose you miss your friends and all.

ANNE   It isn't just . . . (*She breaks off and stares up at him for a second*) Isn't it funny, you and I? Here we've been seeing each other every minute for almost a year and a half, and this is the first time we've ever really talked. It helps a lot to have someone to talk to, don't you think? It helps you to let off steam.

PETER   (*edging to the door*) Well, any time you want to let off steam, you can come into my room.

ANNE   (*rising and following him*) I can get up an awful lot of steam. You'll have to be careful how you say that.

PETER   It's all right with me.

ANNE   Do you mean it?

PETER   I said it, didn't I?

(ANNE *stands in her doorway looking after* PETER, *who stands for a moment looking back at* ANNE *then turns and opens the door.* ANNE'S VOICE *is heard in the darkness, faintly at first, then with growing strength.*)

ANNE'S VOICE   We've had bad news. The people from whom Miep got our ration books have been arrested. So we have had to cut down on our food. Our stomachs are so empty that they rumble and make strange noises, all in different keys. Mr Van Daan's is deep and low, like a bass fiddle. Mine is high, whistling like a flute. As we all sit around waiting for supper, it's like an orchestra tuning up. It only needs Toscanini to raise his baton and we'd be off in the Ride of the Valkyries. Monday, the sixth of March, nineteen forty-four. Mr Kraler is in the hospital. It seems he has ulcers. Pim says we are his ulcers. Miep has to run the business and us, too. The Americans have landed on the southern tip of Italy. Father looks for a quick finish to the war. Mr Dussel is waiting every day for the warehouse man to demand more money. Have I been skipping too much from one subject to another? I can't help it. I feel that spring is coming. (ANNE'S VOICE *starts to fade.*) I feel it in my whole body and soul. I feel utterly confused. I am longing – so longing – for everything – for friends – for someone to talk to – someone who understands – someone young, who feels as I do.

Scene Two

The same. March 1944. Evening. It is after supper.

Outside we hear the sound of children playing. The grown-ups with the exception of MR VAN DAAN, *are all in the centre room. He is sitting in the attic room, working on a piece of embroidery in an embroidery frame. All the lamps are lit.* PETER *is sitting in his room, on the foot of his bed, combing his hair before a small mirror set up on the window-seat. During the ensuing scene, he puts on his tie, polishes his shoes, brushes his coat, puts it on, then makes certain that his room is neat. He is preparing for a visit from* ANNE. *The blackout curtain covers the skylight. A group of photographs is now on the wall. One is slightly tilted.* ANNE *and* MARGOT *are in* ANNE'S *room.* ANNE, *too, is getting dressed. She stands in her slip before the mirror on the dressing-table, putting up her hair.* MARGOT *is seated on* ANNE'S *bed, stitching the waistband of a skirt for* ANNE *to wear. The sewing basket is beside her.* DUSSEL *strides down to* MRS FRANK *and looks at her, appealing for help.* MRS FRANK *becomes more absorbed in her sewing.* DUSSEL *stamps across to the couch.* MRS FRANK *looks unhappily after him.* DUSSEL *sits on the couch, pops up immediately, goes to the door of the room and raps sharply on it.*

ANNE (*calling*) No, no, Mr Dussel. I am not dressed yet.

(DUSSEL, *furious, moves to the couch, sits on it and buries his head in his hands.* ANNE *turns to* MARGOT.)

How is that? How does that look?

MARGOT Fine.

ANNE   You didn't even look.

MARGOT   Of course I did. It's fine.

ANNE   Margot, tell me, am I terribly ugly?

(MRS FRANK, *feeling sorry for* DUSSEL, *motions him to be patient. He resumes his seat.*)

MARGOT   Oh, stop fishing.

ANNE   No. No. Tell me.

MARGOT   Of course you're not. You've got nice eyes – and a lot of animation, and . . .

ANNE   (*dryly*) A little vague, aren't you? (*She reaches over, takes a brassière of* MARGOT'S *out of the sewing basket and tries it on over her slip.*)

MRS FRANK   (*knocking at the door*) May I come in?

MARGOT   Come in, Mother.

(MRS FRANK *goes into the room and closes the door behind her.*)

MRS FRANK   Mr Dussel's impatient to get in here.

ANNE   Heavens, he takes the room for himself the entire day.

MRS FRANK   (*gently*) Anne, dear, you're not going in again tonight to see Peter?

ANNE   (*with dignity*) That is my intention. (*She turns to the
            mirror to study the effect of the brassière.*)

MRS FRANK   But you've already spent a great deal of time in there
            today.

ANNE   I was in there exactly twice. Once to get the
            dictionary, and then three-quarters of an hour before
            supper. (*She turns to view herself from another
            angle.*)

MRS FRANK   Aren't you afraid you're disturbing him?

ANNE   Mother, I have some intuition.

MRS FRANK   Then may I ask you this much, Anne. Please don't shut
            the door when you go in.

ANNE   You sound like Mrs Van Daan. (*She throws the
            brassière back in the sewing basket, picks up her
            blouse and puts it on.*)

MRS FRANK   No. No. I don't mean to suggest anything wrong. I only
            wish that you wouldn't expose yourself to criticism –
            that you wouldn't give Mrs Van Daan the opportunity
            to be unpleasant.

ANNE   Mrs Van Daan doesn't need an opportunity to be
            unpleasant.

MRS FRANK   Everyone's on edge, worried about Mr Kraler. This is
            one more thing ...

ANNE   I'm sorry, Mother. I'm going to Peter's room. I'm not
            going to let Petronella Van Daan spoil our friendship.

(MRS FRANK *hesitates a second, then goes into the centre room, closes the door after her, indicates to* DUSSEL *that it will not be long now, gets a pack of cards, then sits and plays solitaire. When* MRS FRANK *leaves,* ANNE *turns to* MARGOT, *indicating she would like to wear her high-heeled shoes.* MARGOT *smiles agreement and* ANNE *hands her a piece of paper from the dressing-table, for* MARGOT *to put into the shoes.* MARGOT *gives the skirt to* ANNE *and slips off her shoes.*)

MARGOT   (*stuffing the paper into the shoes*) Why don't you two talk in the main room? It'd save a lot of trouble. It's hard on mother, having to listen to those remarks from Mrs Van Daan and not say a word.

ANNE   (*putting on the skirt*) Why doesn't she say a word? I think it's ridiculuos to take it and take it.

MARGOT   You don't understand mother at all, do you? She can't talk back. She's not like you. It's just not in her nature to fight back.

ANNE   Anyway – the only one I worry about is you. I feel awfully guilty about you. (*She sits on the stool, putting on* MARGOT'S *high-heeled shoes.*)

MARGOT   What about?

ANNE   I mean, every time I go into Peter's room, I have a feeling I may be hurting you.

(MARGOT *shakes her head.* ANNE *rises then sits on the foot of the bed with* MARGOT.)

I know if it were me, I'd be wild. I'd be desperately jealous, if it were me.

MARGOT   Well, I'm not.

ANNE   You don't feel badly? Really? Truly? You're not jealous?

MARGOT   Of course I'm jealous – jealous that you've got
something to get up in the morning for – but jealous of
you and Peter? No.

ANNE   (*rising and moving to the mirror*) Maybe there's
nothing to be jealous of. Maybe he doesn't really like
me. Maybe I'm just taking the place of his cat. (*She
picks up a pair of short white gloves and puts them
on.*) Wouldn't you like to come in with us?

MARGOT   I have a book.

(DUSSEL *can stand it no longer. He jumps up, goes to
the door and knocks sharply.*)

DUSSEL   Will you please let me in my room.

ANNE   Just a minute, dear, dear Mr Dussel. (*She picks up her
mother's pink shawl, adjusts it elegantly over her
shoulders, gives a last look in the mirror, then goes to
the door and turns to* MARGOT.)

Well, here I go – to run the gauntlet. (*She goes into the
centre room.* MARGOT *switches off the pendant and
goes into the centre room.*)

DUSSEL   (*sarcastically*) Thank you so much.

(ANNE *gives* DUSSEL *a dignified bow. He goes into the room and closes the door.* ANNE *crosses below the table, trying to appear very sophisticated.*)

MRS V. DAAN My God, look at her!

(ANNE *pays no attention and continues towards* PETER'S *room.* MARGOT'S *heels give her a bit of trouble, but her head is high.* MARGOT *gets her crossword puzzle book and pencil, crosses to the couch, adjusts the lamp, then sits on the couch and fills in a puzzle.* ANNE *knocks at* PETER'S *door.* PETER *makes a quick check to see all is in order.*)

I don't know what good it is to have a son. I never see him. He wouldn't care if I killed myself.

(PETER *opens the door and stands aside for* ANNE *to enter. She rises.*)

Just a minute, Anne. I'd like to say a few words to my son. Do you mind? Peter, I don't want you staying up till all hours tonight. You've got to have your sleep. You're a growing boy. You hear?

MRS FRANK Anne won't stay late. She's going to bed promptly at nine. Aren't you, Anne?

ANNE Yes, Mother. (*To* MRS VAN DAAN. *Too sweetly.*) May we go now?

(*The sound of the children playing outside fades.*)

MRS V. DAAN Are you asking me? I didn't know I had anything to say about it.

MRS FRANK Listen for the chimes, Anne dear.

(PETER *and* ANNE *go into the room and close the door.*)

MRS V. DAAN   In my day it was the boys who called on the girls.

MRS FRANK   You know how young people like to feel that they have secrets. Peter's room is the only place where they can talk.

(*Twilight falls.*)

MRS V. DAAN   Talk! That's not what they called it when I was young.

ANNE   Aren't they awful? Aren't they impossible? Treating us as if we're still in the nursery.

PETER   Don't let it bother you. It doesn't bother me.

ANNE   I suppose you can't really blame them – (*She sits on the foot of* PETER'S *bed.*) they think back to what they were like at our age. They don't realize how much more advanced we are. When I think what wonderful discussions we've had ... Oh, I forgot. I was going to bring you some more pictures.

(PETER *takes out a bottle of orange squash and two glasses from his box-table.*)

PETER   Oh, these are fine, thanks.

ANNE   Don't you want some more? Miep just brought me some new ones.

PETER   Maybe later. (*He sits on the window-seat, facing* ANNE, *hands her a glass, pours some orange in it, then takes some for himself.*)

ANNE   (*looking at one of the photographs*) I remember when I got that – I won it. I bet Jopie that I could eat five ice-cream cones. We'd all been playing ping-pong. We used to have heavenly times – we'd finish up with ice cream at the *Delphi* or the *Oasis*, where Jews were allowed. There'd always be a lot of boys – we'd laugh and joke. I'd like to go back to it for a few days or a week. But after that I know I'd be bored to death. I think more seriously about life, now. I want to be a journalist – or something. I love to write. What do you want to do?

PETER   I thought I might go off some place – work on a farm or something – some job that doesn't take much brains.

ANNE   You shouldn't talk that way. You've got the most awful inferiority complex.

PETER   I know I'm not smart.

ANNE   That isn't true. You're much better than I am in dozens of things – arithmetic and algebra and ... Well, you're a million times better than I am in algebra. (*With sudden directness.*) You like Margot, don't you? Right from the start you liked her, liked her much better than me.

PETER   (*uncomfortably*) Oh, I don't know.

ANNE   It's all right. Everyone feels that way. Margot's so good. She's sweet and bright and beautiful, and I'm not.

PETER   I wouldn't say that.

ANNE   Oh, no, I'm not. I know that. I know quite well that I'm not a beauty. I never have been and never shall be.

PETER   I don't agree at all. I think you're pretty.

ANNE   That's not true.

PETER   And another thing. You've changed – from at first, I mean.

ANNE   I have?

PETER   I used to think you were awful noisy.

ANNE   (*eagerly*) And what do you think now, Peter? How have I changed?

PETER   Well – er – you're – quieter.

ANNE   (*amused*) I'm glad you don't just hate me.

PETER   I never said that.

ANNE   I bet when you get out of here you'll never think of me again.

PETER   That's crazy.

ANNE   When you get back with all of your friends, you're going to say – 'Now what did I ever see in that Mrs Quack Quack?'

PETER   I haven't got any friends.

ANNE   Oh, Peter, of course you have. Everyone has friends.

PETER Not me. I don't want any. I get along all right without them.

ANNE Does that mean you can get along without me? I think of myself as your friend.

PETER No. If they were all like you, it'd be different. (*He realizes what he has said. To cover his embarrassment he hurriedly picks up the glasses and bottle and returns them to the box-table.*)

(*There is a second's silence and then* ANNE *speaks, hesitantly and shyly. She cannot look at* PETER.)

ANNE Peter, did you ever kiss a girl?

PETER Yes. Once.

(ANNE *looks quickly back over her shoulder at him.*)

ANNE (*to cover her feelings*) That picture's crooked. (*She looks away.*)

(PETER *straightens the picture.*)

Was she pretty?

PETER Huh?

ANNE The girl that you kissed.

PETER I don't know. I was blindfolded. (*He resumes his place opposite her.*) It was at a party. One of those kissing games.

ANNE   (*relieved*) Oh, I don't suppose that really counts, does it?

PETER   It didn't with me.

ANNE   I've been kissed twice. Once a man I'd never seen before kissed me on the cheek when he picked me up off the ice and I was crying. And the other was Mr Koophuis, a friend of father's who kissed my hand. You wouldn't say those counted, would you?

PETER   I wouldn't say so.

ANNE   I know almost for certain that Margot would never kiss anyone unless she was engaged to them. And I'm sure, too, that mother never touched a man before Pim. But I don't know – things are so different now. What do you think? Do you think a girl shouldn't kiss anyone except if she's engaged or something? It's so hard to try to think what to do, when here we are with the whole world falling around our ears and you think – well – you don't know what's going to happen tomorrow, and . . . What do you think?

PETER   I suppose it'd depend on the girl. Some girls, anything they do's wrong. But others – well – it wouldn't necessarily be wrong with them. (The carillon chimes and strikes nine o'clock.) I've always thought that when two people . . .

ANNE   Nine o'clock. I have to go.

PETER   That's right.

ANNE   (*without moving*) Good night.

(*Their faces are close together. There is a second's pause, then* PETER, *too shy to kiss* ANNE, *rises and moves away.*)

PETER   You won't let them stop you coming?

ANNE   No. (*She rises, moves to the door and turns.*) Some time I might bring my diary. There are so many things in it that I want to talk over with you. There's a lot about you.

PETER   What kind of things?

ANNE   I wouldn't want you to see some of it. I thought you were a nothing, just the way you thought about me.

PETER   Did you change your mind, the way I changed my mind about you?

ANNE   Well – you'll see . . .

(*For a second* ANNE *stands looking up at* PETER, *longing for him to kiss her. As he makes no move, she turns to go. Then suddenly he grabs her and, turning her around, holds her awkwardly in his arms, kissing her on the cheek.* ANNE, *dazed, floats slowly out of the room. She stands for a minute, her back to the people in the centre room, shutting the door behind her. After a moment her poise returns, and with a sophisticated motion she flips one end of her shawl back over her shoulder. Then she goes to* MR *and* MRS FRANK *and silently kisses them good night.* MR *and* MRS FRANK *murmur their 'good nights'.* ANNE *crosses to* MARGOT, *kisses her, then goes to her door.* MR *and* MRS FRANK *stop their game and watch* ANNE. ANNE *is suddenly aware of* MRS VAN DAAN *at the sink, goes quickly to her, takes* MRS VAN

DAAN'S *face in her hands, and kisses first on one cheek
and then on the other, then goes into her room and
closes the door.* MRS VAN DAAN *moves slowly above the
table and watches* ANNE *go, then looks slowly towards*
PETER'S *room. Her suspicions are confirmed.* MR *and*
MRS FRANK *return to their game.*)

MRS V. DAAN   (*knowingly*) Ah, hah!

(*We hear* ANNE'S VOICE, *faintly at first, then with
growing strength.*)

ANNE'S VOICE   By this time we all know each other so well that if
anyone starts to tell a story, the rest can finish it for
him. We're having to cut down still further on our
meals. What makes it worse, the rats have been at work
again. They've carried off some of our precious food.
Even Mr Dussel wishes now that Mouschi was here.
Thursday, the twentieth of April, nineteen forty-four.
Invasion fever is mounting every day. Miep tells us that
people outside talk of nothing else. For myself, life has
become much more pleasant. I often go to Peter's
room after supper. Oh, don't think I'm in love, because
I'm not. But it does make life more bearable to have
someone with whom you can exchange views. No
more tonight. PS I must be honest. I must confess that I
actually live for the next meeting. Is there anything
lovelier than to sit under the skylight and feel the sun
on your cheeks and have a darling boy in your arms? I
admit now that I'm glad the Van Daans had a son and
not a daughter. (ANNE'S VOICE *fades out.*) I've outgrown
another dress. That's the third. I'm having to wear
Margot's clothes after all. I'm working hard on my
French – and am now reading *La Belle Nivernaise.*

Scene Three

The same. June 1944. Night.

Everyone is in bed and all is quiet. A dim cool light falls through the skylight. We can faintly see MR *and* MRS FRANK *and* ANNE *in their beds.* MARGOT *sleeps behind the drawn curtain. Suddenly in the attic room a match flares up for a moment and then is quickly put out.* MR VAN DAAN, *in bare feet, dressed in underwear and trousers, is dimly seen coming stealthily down the attic stairs and into the centre room. He goes to the food cupboard under the sink and again lights a match. Then he cautiously opens the cupboard and takes out a half loaf of bread. As he closes the cupboard, it creaks. He stands rigid.* MRS FRANK *sits up in bed and sees* MR VAN DAAN.

MRS FRANK   (*screaming*) Otto! Otto! Come quick.

(*The others wake and hurriedly get up.*)

MR FRANK   What is it? What's happened?

(MR VAN DAAN *starts for the stairs.*)

MRS FRANK   (*rushing to* MR VAN DAAN) He's stealing the food.

(DUSSEL *dashes out of his room towards* MR VAN DAAN. ANNE *follows, after throwing a skirt over her shoulders like a shawl.*)

DUSSEL   You! You! Give me that.

(PETER *comes out of his room.*)

MRS V. DAAN   (*getting out of bed*) Putti – Putti – what is it?

(*The following speeches overlap.*)

DUSSEL (*grabbing the bread*) You dirty thief –

(MR VAN DAAN *backs away*.)

– stealing food – you good-for-nothing . . .

(MARGOT *switches on the pendant*.)

MR FRANK (*putting his arms round* DUSSEL'S *waist and tugging*) Mr Dussel. For God's sake! Help me, Peter.

(PETER *works down behind his father and pulls at his shoulders*.)

PETER (*to* DUSSEL) Let him go. Let go.

(DUSSEL *and* MR FRANK *give a tug that pulls* MR VAN DAAN *to his knees*. DUSSEL *has the bread*. MR VAN DAAN *rises quickly and retreats*.)

DUSSEL You greedy, selfish . . .

MRS V. DAAN (*coming down the attic stairs*) Putti – what is it?

(*All of* MRS FRANK'S *gentleness, her self-control is gone. She is outraged, in a frenzy of indignation*.)

MRS FRANK The bread! He was stealing the bread.

(DUSSEL *stands by the table and places the bread on it*. PETER, *humiliated, sits on the stairs*.)

DUSSEL It was you, and all the time we thought it was the rats.

MR FRANK Mr Van Daan, how could you?

MR V. DAAN   I'm hungry.

MRS FRANK   (*with righteous rage*) We're all of us hungry. I see the children getting thinner and thinner. Your own son Peter – I've heard him moan in his sleep, he's so hungry. And you come in the night and steal food that should go to them – to the children.

MRS V. DAAN   He needs more food than the rest of us. He's used to more. He's a big man.

MRS FRANK   (*turning on* MRS VAN DAAN) And you – you're worse than he is. You're a mother, and yet you sacrifice your child to this man – this – this . . .

MR FRANK   Edith! Edith!

(MARGOT *picks up the shawl from the chair and puts it over* MRS FRANK'S *shoulders*.)

MRS FRANK   (*paying no attention; to* MRS VAN DAAN) Don't think I haven't seen you. Always saving the choicest bits for him. I've watched you day after day and I've held my tongue. But not any longer. Not after this. Now, I want him to go. I want him to get out of here. (*She moves up C.*)

MR FRANK } (*together*) Edith!
MR V. DAAN }   Get out of here?

MRS V. DAAN   (*sinking into the chair*) What do you mean?

MRS FRANK   Just that. Take your things and get out.

MR FRANK   (*to his wife*) You're speaking in anger. You cannot mean what you are saying.

MRS FRANK   I mean exactly that.

MR FRANK   For two long years we have lived here, side by side. We have respected each other's rights – we have managed to live in peace. Are we now going to throw it all away?

(MR VAN DAAN *becomes ill, fears that he is going to retch and rises.*)

I know this will never happen again, will it, Mr Van Daan?

MR V. DAAN   No, No. (*Holding his mouth and stomach, he moves towards the WC.*)

(ANNE *puts her arms around* MR VAN DAAN *and helps him up the steps.* MR VAN DAAN *goes into the WC and switches on the light.* MRS VAN DAAN *rises to help, but they have gone. She moves to the couch, takes a cover from the bed and puts it around her shoulders.*)

MRS FRANK   He steals once! He'll steal again.

MR FRANK   Edith, please! Let us be calm. We'll all go to our rooms – and afterwards we'll sit down quietly and talk this out – we'll find some way ...

MRS FRANK   No! No! No more talk. I want them to leave.

(MR FRANK *realizes he cannot reason with his wife, makes a hopeless gesture and goes to* ANNE *and* MARGOT.)

MRS V. DAAN   You'd put us out, on the streets?

MRS FRANK   There are other hiding places.

MRS V. DAAN   A cellar – a closet. I know. And we have no money left even to pay for that.

MRS FRANK   I'll give you money. Out of my own pocket I'll give it gladly.

MRS V. DAAN   Mr Frank, you told Putti you'd never forget what he'd done for you when you came to Amsterdam. You said you could never repay him, that you . . .

MRS FRANK   (*counting out money*) If my husband had any obligation to you, he's paid it, over and over.

MR FRANK   Edith, I've never seen you like this before. I don't know you.

MRS FRANK   I should have spoken out long ago.

DUSSEL   You can't be nice to some people.

MRS V. DAAN   (*to* DUSSEL) There would have been plenty for all of us, if *you* hadn't come in here.

MR FRANK   We don't need the Nazis to destroy us. We're destroying ourselves. (*He sits, with his head in his hands.*)

MRS FRANK   (*turning to* MRS VAN DAAN) Give this to Miep. She'll find you a place. (*She forces the money into* MRS VAN DAAN'S *hand.*)

ANNE   Mother, you're not putting *Peter* out. Peter hasn't done anything.

MRS FRANK   He'll stay, of course. When I say the children, I mean
             Peter, too.

PETER   (*rising*) I'd have to go if father goes.

             (MR VAN DAAN *switches out the WC light and comes
             into the centre room.* MRS VAN DAAN *hurries to him and
             takes him to the couch where he sits, then she goes to
             the sink, gets some water and bathes her husband's
             face.*)

MRS FRANK   (*to* PETER) He's no father to you – that man. He doesn't
             know what it is to be a father.

PETER   I wouldn't feel right. I couldn't stay.

MRS FRANK   Very well, then. I'm sorry.

ANNE   (*rushing to* PETER) No, Peter! No!

             (PETER *goes into his room, closes the door and goes
             into the closet area.* ANNE *turns to her mother, crying.*)

             I don't care about the food. They can have mine. I
             don't want it. Only don't send them away. It'll be
             daylight soon. They'll be caught.

MARGOT   Please, Mother!

MRS FRANK   They're not going now. They'll stay here until Miep
             finds them a hiding-place. (*To* MRS VAN DAAN.) But one
             thing I insist on. He must never come down here again.
             He must never come to this room where the food is
             stored. We'll divide what we have – an equal share for
             each.

(DUSSEL *rises, crosses to the cupboard under the sink and takes a bag of potatoes from it.*)

You can cook it here and take it up to him. (*She moves up C.*)

(DUSSEL *puts the potatoes on the table.*)

MARGOT   Oh, no! No. We haven't sunk so far that we're going to fight over a handful of rotten potatoes.

DUSSEL   (*dividing the potatoes into piles*) Mrs Frank – Mr Frank – Margot – Anne – Peter – Mrs Van Daan – Mr Van Daan – myself – Mrs Frank . . .

(*The buzzer sounds* MIEP'S *signal. All freeze for an instant.*)

MR FRANK   (*rising quickly*) It's Miep.

MARGOT   At this hour?

MRS FRANK   It must be trouble.

MR FRANK   (*stopping and turning; to* DUSSEL) I beg you, don't let her see a thing like this.

DUSSEL   (*who has been counting without stopping*) Anne – Peter – Mrs Van Daan – Mr Van Daan – myself – Mrs Frank . . .

MARGOT   (*to* DUSSEL) Stop it! Stop it! (MR FRANK *goes down the stair-well and opens the door.*)

DUSSEL   Mr Frank – Margot – Anne – Peter – Mrs Van Daan – Mr Van Daan – myself – Mrs Frank . . .

MRS V. DAAN   (*pointing at the potato piles*) You're keeping the big
ones for yourself. All the big ones – look at the size of
that – and that . . .

(DUSSEL *continues with his dividing.* PETER, *with his
shirt and trousers on, comes from his room and stops
just outside the door.*)

MARGOT   (*to* DUSSEL) Stop it! Stop it!

MIEP   (*off; excited*) Mr Frank – the most wonderful news –
the invasion has begun.

MR FRANK   (*off*) No! No!

(MIEP *runs up the stairwell, ahead of* MR FRANK. *She has
a man's raincoat over her nightclothes, and carries a
bunch of flowers.*)

MIEP   Did you hear that everybody? Did you hear what I said?
The invasion has begun.

(*They all stare at* MIEP, *unable to grasp what she is
telling them.* MR FRANK *comes up the stairwell.*)

The invasion!

(PETER *is the first to recover his wits.*)

PETER   Where?

MIEP   It began early this morning.

(*As* MIEP *speaks, the others, all except* MR VAN DAAN,
crowd around her, listening tensely.)

MRS FRANK   How do you know?

MIEP   The radio. The BBC. They said they landed on the coast of Normandy.

PETER   The British?

MIEP   British, Americans, French, Dutch, Poles, Norwegians – all of them. More than four thousand ships.

(*As* MIEP *goes on, the realization of what is happening begins to come to them, and everyone goes crazy with excitement.*)

Churchill spoke, and General Eisenhower. 'D-Day' they call it.

(*A wild demonstration takes place.* PETER *rushes to the kitchen area and grabs a frying pan.* ANNE *follows him.* PETER *starts to march around the room, followed by* ANNE, *and then by* MARGOT. *They circle the table, singing the Dutch National Anthem. They dum-ta-dum the melody, not using the words.* MIEP *gives* MARGOT *the bunch of flowers as* MARGOT *passes her.* PETER *pounds out the beat of the music on the frying pan.* PETER *and* ANNE *end up inspecting the map hanging above the mantelpiece.* MARGOT *distributes flowers to everyone. During this the grown-ups embrace each other. All enmities are forgotten in the exhilaration of the wonderful news.* MRS FRANK *hugs* MR VAN DAAN, *as* MR FRANK *hugs* MIEP *and* MRS VAN DAAN.)

MR FRANK   Thank God it's come.

MRS V. DAAN   At last.

(MRS FRANK *turns from* MR VAN DAAN *to go to* MIEP *and* MR FRANK. *Only* MR VAN DAAN *does not join in the*

excitement. He is too ashamed of himself. MRS FRANK
meets MRS VAN DAAN *as* MRS VAN DAAN *is going over to
embrace her husband. The two women hug each other
with warm affection, then* MRS FRANK *hugs* MIEP *and* MR
FRANK. MRS VAN DAAN *gives her husband an ecstatic
embrace, then moves to* DUSSEL. MR VAN DAAN *sits too
heartbroken to rejoice with the rest. As* MRS VAN DAAN
goes up to hug DUSSEL, MRS FRANK *has the same thought
and the two women do a little dance of jubiliation
with him.*)

MIEP   (*at the stairwell*) I'm going to tell Mr Kraler – this'll be
better than any blood transfusion.

MR FRANK   (*stopping* MIEP) What part of Normandy did they land,
did they say?

MIEP   Normandy – that's all I know now. I'll be up the minute
I hear some more. (MIEP *exits quickly down the stairwell.*)

MR FRANK   (*taking his wife in his arms*) What did I tell you! What
did I tell you!

(MRS FRANK *indicates that* MR FRANK *has forgotten to
bolt the door after* MIEP, *and he hurries down the
stairwell.* MARGOT *goes to give a flower to* MR VAN DAAN.
*As she holds it out to him, he suddenly breaks into a
convulsive sob.* MRS VAN DAAN *rushes to her husband
and sits above him on the couch, trying to comfort
him.* MARGOT, *not understanding the outburst,
retreats.*)

MRS V. DAAN   Putti! Putti! What is it? What happened?

MR V. DAAN   Please. I'm so ashamed.

(MRS FRANK *comes up the stairwell.*)

DUSSEL   Oh, for God's sake . . . (*He goes to the table and replaces the potatoes in the bag.*)

MRS V. DAAN   Don't, Putti.

MARGOT   It doesn't matter, now.

MR FRANK   Didn't you hear what Miep said? The invasion has come. We're going to be liberated. This is a time to celebrate. (*He gets the cognac and a glass, which he brings to the table, where he pours a stiff drink.*)

MR V. DAAN   To steal bread from children.

MRS FRANK   We've all done things that we're ashamed of.

ANNE   Look at me, the way I've treated mother – so mean and horrid to her.

MRS FRANK   No, Anneline, no.

ANNE   (*moving to* MRS FRANK *and putting her arms around her*) Oh, Mother, I was. I was awful.

MR V. DAAN   Not like me. No-one is as bad as me.

DUSSEL   Stop it now! Let's be happy.

MR FRANK   (*giving the glass of cognac to* MR VAN DAAN) Here! Here! Schnapps! L'chaim!

(MR VAN DAAN *takes the cognac. They all watch him.* ANNE *puts up her fingers in a V-for-Victory sign. As* MR

VAN DAAN *gives a faint smile and an answering V-sign,
they are startled to hear a loud wailing sob from
behind them. They all look over to* MRS FRANK *who,
stricken with remorse, sinks into the chair down L
and wails.*)

Edith . . .

(*He pats her hand.* ANNE *and* MARGOT *rush across,
kneel at* MRS FRANK'S *feet and comfort her.*)

MRS FRANK   (*through her sobs*) When I think of the terrible things I
said . . .

(MR VAN DAAN *rises, crosses to* MRS FRANK *and makes a
V-sign.*)

MR V. DAAN   (*earnestly*) No! No! You were right.

MRS FRANK   (*still sobbing*) That I should speak that way to you –
our friends – our guests . . .

DUSSEL   Stop it! You're spoiling – the whole invasion.

(ANNE'S VOICE *is heard faintly at first, and then with
growing strength.*)

ANNE'S VOICE   We're all in much better spirits these days. There's still
excellent news of the invasion. The best part about it is
that I have a feeling that friends are coming. Who
knows? Maybe I'll be back in school by autumn. Ha, ha!
The joke is on us. The warehouse man doesn't know a
thing and we are paying him all that money.
Wednesday, the second of July, nineteen forty-four.
The invasion seems temporarily to be bogged down.
Mr Kraler has to have an operation, which looks bad.

The Gestapo have found the radio that was stolen. Mr
Dussel says they'll trace it back and back to the thief,
and then, it's just a matter of time till they get to us.
Everyone is low. Even poor Pim can't raise their spirits.
I have often been downcast myself – but never in
despair. I can shake off everything if I write. But – and
that is the great question – will I ever be able to write
well? I want to so much. I want to go on living even
after my death. (ANNE'S VOICE *fades.*) Another birthday
has gone by, so now I am fifteen. Already I know what I
want. I have a goal, an opinion.

Scene Four

The same. July 1944. Afternoon.

When the lights come up, everyone but MARGOT *is in
the centre room. There is a sense of great tension. In
the distance a German military band is heard in a
rendition of some Viennese waltzes.* DUSSEL *is standing
at the window looking down fixedly at the street
below.* MARGOT *is at the dressing-table in* ANNE'S *room.
The table-lamp is on.* PETER *is with his copybooks,
trying to do his lessons.* ANNE *sits writing in her diary.*
MRS VAN DAAN *is seated on the couch, a book beside her,
her eyes on* MR FRANK. MRS FRANK *is looking fearfully
towards the stairwell.* MR VAN DAAN *is pacing. He
reverses and goes to* MR FRANK. *There is no reaction
from* MR FRANK *so* MR VAN DAAN *paces again. The
telephone in the office below begins to ring.* MR VAN
DAAN *turns and looks towards the stairwell.* MRS FRANK
*stands rigid, tight with fear. They all freeze and listen
intently.* DUSSEL *rushes down to* MR FRANK. *The
telephone continues to ring.*

DUSSEL   There is goes again, the telephone. Mr Frank, do you
         hear?

MR FRANK   (*quietly*) Yes. I hear.

DUSSEL   (*pleading and insistent*) But this is the third time, Mr
         Frank. The third time in quick succession. It's a signal. I
         tell you it's Miep, trying to warn us. For some reason
         she can't come to us and she's trying to warn us of
         something.

MR FRANK   Please. Please.

MR V. DAAN   (*to* DUSSEL) You're wasting your breath.

DUSSEL   Something has happened, Mr Frank. For three days now
         Miep hasn't been to see us. And today not a man has
         come to work. There hasn't been a sound in the
         building.

MRS FRANK   Perhaps it's Sunday. We may have lost track of the days.

MR V. DAAN   (*to* ANNE) You with the diary there. What day is it?

         (ANNE *closes the diary so he cannot read what she is
         writing.*)

DUSSEL   I don't lose track of the days. I know exactly what day
         it is. It's Friday, the fourth of August. Friday, and not a
         man at work. (*He rushes down to* MR FRANK, *pleading
         with him, almost in tears.*) I tell you Mr Kraler's dead.
         That's the only explanation. He's dead and they've
         closed down the building, and Miep's trying to tell us.

MR FRANK   She'd never telephone us.

DUSSEL   Mr Frank, answer that. I beg you, answer it.

MR FRANK   No.

MR V. DAAN   Just pick it up and listen. You don't have to speak. Just listen and see if it's Miep.

DUSSEL   For God's sake – I ask you.

MR FRANK   No. I've told you 'no'. I'll do nothing that might let anyone know we're in the building.

PETER   Mr Frank's right.

MR V. DAAN   There's no need to tell us what side you're on.

MR FRANK   If we wait patiently, quietly, I believe that help will come.

(*There is silence for a minute as they all listen to the telephone ringing.*)

DUSSEL   I'm going down. (*He rushes down the stairwell.* MR FRANK *rises and tries ineffectually to stop him. When* DUSSEL *reaches the outside door, the telephone stops, but he rushes out anyway.* MR FRANK *waits tensely, wondering if he should go after* DUSSEL. MRS FRANK *moves to the stairwell and gazes tensely down.* PETER *rises. After a moment* DUSSEL *returns, shuts the door and comes up the stairs.*)

Too late.

(MR FRANK *looks out of the edge of the blackout curtain, then goes to* MARGOT. DUSSEL *goes to the window.* MRS FRANK *goes to the sink, gets some potatoes and a knife, sits on the padded stool above the stove and peels the potatoes.*)

MR V. DAAN So we just wait here until we die.

MRS V. DAAN I can't stand it! I'll kill myself. I'll kill myself.

MR V. DAAN For God's sake, stop it!

MRS V. DAAN I think you'd be glad if I did. I think you want me to die.

MR V. DAAN Whose fault is it we're here?

(MRS VAN DAAN *covers her ears.*)

We could have been safe somewhere – in America or Switzerland.

(MRS VAN DAAN *rises and crosses to the attic stairs. He follows* MRS VAN DAAN, *shouting.*)

But no! No! You wouldn't leave when I wanted to. You couldn't leave your things. You couldn't leave your precious furniture. (*He grabs her arm.*)

MRS V. DAAN (*shaking him off*) Don't touch me! (*She goes quickly up to the attic room.*)

(MR VAN DAAN *follows slowly after her.* PETER, *humiliated and desperate, goes into his room.* ANNE, *deeply concerned, looks after him.* PETER *throws himself face down on his bed.* MRS VAN DAAN, *sobbing quietly, lies on her bed.* MR FRANK *comes into the centre*

*room, goes to the couch, sits, picks up a book and tries
to read.* ANNE *rises and goes quietly, closing the door
behind her. She sits on the edge of the bed, leans over*
PETER, *holds him in her arms and tries to bring him out
of his despair.* PETER *is too unhappy to respond.*)

ANNE   (*after a pause; looking up through the skylight*) Look,
Peter, the sky. What a lovely day. Aren't the clouds
beautiful? You know what I do when it seems as if I
couldn't stand being cooped up for one more minute? I
think myself out. I think myself on a walk in the park
where I used to go with Pim. Where the daffodils and
the crocuses and the violets grow down the slopes.
You know the most wonderful thing about *thinking*
yourself out? You can have it any way you like. You can
have roses and violets and chrysanthemums all
blooming at the same time. It's funny – I used to take it
all for granted – and now, I've gone crazy about
everything to do with nature. Haven't you?

PETER   I've just gone crazy. I think if something doesn't
happen soon – if we don't get out of here . . . I can't
stand much more of it.

ANNE   I wish you had a religion, Peter.

PETER   No thanks. Not me.

ANNE   Oh, I don't mean you have to be Orthodox – or believe
in heaven and hell and purgatory and things – I just
mean some religion – it doesn't matter what. Just to
believe in something. When I think of all that's out there
– the trees – and flowers – and seagulls – when I think
of the dearness of you, Peter – and the goodness of the
people we know – Mr Kraler, Miep, Dirk, the vegetable

man, all risking their lives for us every day – when I think of these good things, I'm not afraid any more – I find myself, and God, and I . . .

PETER That's fine! But when I begin to think, I get mad. Look at us, hiding out for two years. Not able to move. Caught here like . . . Waiting for them to come and get us – and all for what?

ANNE We're not the only people that've had to suffer. There've always been people that've had to – sometimes one race – sometimes another – and yet . . .

PETER That doesn't make me feel any better.

ANNE I know it's terrible, trying to have any faith – when people are doing such horrible . . . (*She gently lifts his face.*) But you know what I sometimes think? I think the world may be going through a phase, the way I was with mother. It'll pass, maybe not for hundreds of years, but some day. I still believe, in spite of everything, that people are really good at heart.

PETER I want to see something now – not a thousand years from now.

ANNE (*moving to him*) But, Peter, if you'd only look at it as part of a great pattern – that we're just a little minute in life . . . (*She breaks off, with a rueful smile.*) Listen to us, going at each other like a couple of stupid grown-ups. (*She holds out her hand to him.* PETER *takes* ANNE'S *hand.*) Look at the sky, now. Isn't it lovely?

(PETER *stands behind* ANNE *with his arms around her. They look up at the sky.*)

Some day, when we're outside again, I'm going to ... (ANNE *breaks off as she hears the sound of a car outside, its brakes squealing as it comes to a sudden stop. The people in the other rooms also become aware of the sound, and all listen tensely.*

Another car outside roars up to a sudden stop. MR FRANK, *book in hand, rises slowly. Everyone is listening, hardly breathing.*

Suddenly a heavy electric bell begins clanging savagely below. ANNE *and* PETER *hurry from the room. She stops just outside the door. He remains on the first step.* MARGOT *hurries into the centre room.*

MRS FRANK *puts down the potatoes.* MRS VAN DAAN *rises and comes fearfully down the attic stairs.* MR VAN DAAN *stays above at the head of the staircase. All eyes are fixed on* MR FRANK, *who crosses slowly and calmly towards the stairwell. He drops the book on the chair. The bell stops.* MR FRANK *turns to the others, making a reassuring gesture, then starts down the stairwell.*

The bell begins another long peal. DUSSEL *comes down and follows* MR FRANK *out.* PETER *follows after* DUSSEL. *The bell stops.* MARGOT *moves to* MRS FRANK *and takes her hand.* MR VAN DAAN *comes down the attic stairs. There is a motionless silence, then* DUSSEL *comes up the stairs with* PETER *close behind.*

The bell starts clanging again. As DUSSEL *gets a step into the room, he slumps to his knees.* PETER *helps him to his feet. Shaking off* PETER'S *help,* DUSSEL *crosses below the table, goes into his room and starts packing. The bell stops.*

From far below, we hear a door being battered down. MR FRANK *returns, bolting the door behind him. The door below crashes. There is a sound of booted footsteps, then another door is battered down. The others look to* MR FRANK *as he stops at the head of the stair-well. He makes a gesture that tells all. A moan escapes* MRS VAN DAAN *and she sags.* PETER *and* MR VAN DAAN *go to* MRS VAN DAAN *and help her to the stool.* MRS FRANK *sinks down into the chair and rests her head forward on the tablecloth.* MARGOT *clings to the back of the chair.* MR FRANK *moves quickly towards the shelves, then stops, turns and speaks to the others.)*

MR FRANK   For the past two years we have lived in fear. Now we can live in hope. (*He picks up a leatherette shopping bag and* ANNE'S *school bag from under the shelves. Moving quickly he gives the school bag to* ANNE. *The other he gives to* MARGOT *and in pantomime asks her where* MRS FRANK'S *bag is.* MARGOT *indicates the WC.* MR FRANK *goes into the WC.*

A pair of boots clump heavily up a flight of stairs to the office below. They sound very near. MR VAN DAAN *starts upstairs to pack.* PETER *moves to* ANNE *and kisses her good-bye, then crossing behind her, he goes into his room to pack.* MARGOT *goes to collect her things. The door buzzer sounds. There is a short pause, followed by another insistent buzz.* MR FRANK *comes from the WC. He carries a bag which he gives to* MRS FRANK. *He then stands holding her hand.* MRS FRANK *raises her head. A rifle butt crashes heavily into the bolted door below. With greater and greater violence the blows fall. Shouted commands are heard.)*

MEN'S VOICES   (*off*) Auf machen! Da drinnen! Auf machen! Schnell! Schnell! Schnell! etc. etc.

(MR *and* MRS FRANK *look over at* ANNE, *who stands, holding her school satchel, looking back at them with a soft reassuring smile. She is no longer a child, but a woman with courage to meet whatever lies ahead. We hear a mighty crash as the door is shattered. After a second* ANNE'S VOICE *is heard.*)

ANNE'S VOICE And so it seems our stay here is over. They are waiting for us now. They've allowed us five minutes to get our things. We can each take a bag and whatever it will hold of clothing. Nothing else. So, dear Diary, that means I must leave you behind. Good-bye for a while. PS Please, please, Miep, or Mr Kraler, or anyone else. If you should find this diary will you please keep it safe for me, because some day I hope . . . (*Her voice stops abruptly. There is a silence.*)

Scene Five

The same. November 1945. Late afternoon.

The rooms are as we saw them at the beginning of the play, except that the chairs and table are upright. KRALER *has joined* MIEP *and* MR FRANK. *We see a great change in* MR FRANK. *He is calm now. His bitterness is gone. Coffee cups are on the table for* KRALER *and* MIEP. KRALER *sits below the table, on the stool.* MIEP *is seated.* MR FRANK *is seated on the couch, with the diary in his hands. His coffee cup is on the table. The sounds of the street organ and children at play are heard. It is early evening.* MR FRANK *slowly turns a few pages of the diary. They are blank.*

MR FRANK No more. (*He closes the diary and puts it on the couch beside him.*)

MIEP I'd gone to the country to find food. When I got back the block was surrounded by police.

KRALER We made it our business to learn how they knew. It was the thief – the thief who told them. (*He indicates to* MIEP *that she should refill the cups.* MIEP *rises, and collects the coffee-pot.*)

MR FRANK It seems strange to say this, that anyone could be happy in a concentration camp. But Anne was happy in the camp in Holland where they first took us. After two years of being shut up in these rooms, she could be out – out in the sunshine and the fresh air that she loved.

MIEP A little more? (MR FRANK *does not really hear* MIEP. *After a moment he realizes what she has said.*)

MR FRANK Yes, thank you.

(MIEP *pours coffee for* MR FRANK, *then refills her own and* KRALER'S *cups, returns the pot and resumes her seat.*)

The news of the war was good. The British and Americans were sweeping through France. We felt sure that they would get to us in time. In September we were told that we were to be shipped to Poland – the men to one camp; the women to another. I was sent to Auschwitz. They went to Belsen. In January we were freed, the few of us who were left. The war wasn't over

yet, so it took us a long time to get home. We'd be sent
here and there behind the lines where we'd be safe.
Each time our train would stop – at a siding, or a
crossing – we'd all get out and go from group to group.
'Where were you?' 'Were you at Belsen?' 'At
Buchenwald?' 'At Mathausen?' 'Is it possible that you
knew my wife?' 'Did you ever see my husband? My son?
My daughter?' That's how I found out about my wife's
death – of Margot, the Van Daans, Peter – Dussel. But
Anne – I still hoped. (*He picks up the diary.*) Yesterday
I went to Rotterdam. I'd heard of a woman there. She'd
been in Belsen with Anne – I know, now. (*He opens
the diary and turns the pages back to find a certain
passage. As* MR FRANK *finds the page we hear* ANNE'S
VOICE).

ANNE'S VOICE   In spite of everything, I still believe that people are
really good at heart.

MR FRANK   She puts me to shame. (MR FRANK *slowly closes the
diary.*)

CURTAIN

QUESTIONS AND EXPLORATIONS

1 Keeping Track

You will need to find out what was happening in Europe at the time of the play. Here is a list of key words and names to research. (The Introduction and Glossary will help.)

Hitler	The Final Solution
Fascism	The Jews
The Nazis	The Holocaust

Act One

Scene One

1 Find out the dates of The Second World War. What is significant about the date at the opening of the play?
2 What is your initial impression of Mr Frank?
3 The diary reads, 'The things got very bad for the Jews.' Find out why.

Scene Two

4 What does Mrs Van Daan mean when she says, 'They've been picked up'?
5 What is the significance of the Star of David? Why do Jews have to wear it on every item of clothing?
6 Make a list of all the rules the families have to stick to. Think about what it would be like to have to stay virtually silent from 8.30–5.30 each day. How would this make you feel?

7   Mr Frank attempts to make life appear as normal as possible. How does he do this?

8   In the first scene in which Anne and Peter meet we are given many clues as to their personalities. How do they compare to one another?

9   Why is Peter so determined to burn his Star of David?

10 Imagine that you are Anne's friend Jopie. Write a diary extract showing your fears.

11 We have learned much about Mr Frank already. List his good qualities. To what extent would you describe him as an optimist?

12 Miep and Mr Kraler are protecting the Franks even though this puts them in great danger. Why do they do this? In the same circumstances, would you?

Scene Three

13 What impression have you formed of Anne so far? Find evidence to show that she has a good sense of humour.

14 How do you think Peter feels about his mother flirting with Mr Frank?

15 Why does Mrs Van Daan care so much about her fur coat? What does it represent to her?

16 'We're all living under terrible tension.' (*page 41*) Look back over the last five pages. What evidence can you find that the characters are beginning to irritate each other? Which characters cope better than others?

17 Mr Frank immediately agrees to take in the Jewish dentist. Mr Van Daan does not think that it is a good idea. Who do you feel is right?

18 How do the Van Daans compare with the Franks in their attitudes?

19 'You make us seem very heroic.' Do you feel that by

helping the Franks Miep and Mr Kraler are heroic? Why do they hate the Nazis so much that they are prepared to risk their lives to help Jews?

Scene Four

20 Do you feel that Mr Dussel will find it difficult to adapt to life in the hideaway? In which ways?

21 Why is Mr Van Daan sneaking to the food cupboard in the middle of the night? What would the others have to say if they caught him?

22 What is your impression of Dussel?

23 What are the dangers if Anne, or anyone else in the Annex, makes a lot of noise? Is Anne a coward?

24 Mr Frank says that all parents can really do is set a good example to their children. 'The rest you must do yourself.' Do you agree?

Scene Five

25 Why does Anne feel guilty? Explain her relationship with her parents as it emerges during this scene.

26 The language used throughout the ceremony is archaic (it sounds very old). Why is this?

27 Even though Dussel is Jewish, he doesn't understand the ceremony. Why is this?

28 When Mrs Frank receives her present from Anne she says, 'This is the most precious gift I've ever had.' What does she mean by this?

29 Make a list of all the gifts Anne gives. Do you feel that they are appropriate for the people who receive them?

30 What does the incident involving the intruder reveal about each of the characters?

31 Obviously the words of the Hanukkah song do not

match the way everyone feels. What emotions do you think Anne and the others have as they sing these words?

Act Two

Scene One

1 How long have the group now been in hiding? What changes have occurred during this period?

2 Mr Van Daan is pleased when Miep and Mr Kraler refuse a piece of cake. Why? What other evidence is there to show that Mr Van Daan is not satisfied with the amount of food he is receiving?

3 What does the incident with the cake show us about the characters?

4 Mrs Van Daan is very protective over her coat. Mr Dussel wonders how she can be 'so silly as to worry about a fur coat in times like this'. With which character do you have more sympathy? Do you feel that Mr Van Daan's real motive for selling it is, as he claims, to help people 'in desperate need of clothing'?

5 Margot says, 'Sometimes I wish the end would come.' Can you understand why she feels this way?

6 Describe the change in the relationship between Anne and Peter.

Scene Two

7 What does Anne mean when she says that she will have to 'run the gauntlet'? Why is she criticized for visiting Peter's room?

Scene Three

8 When Mr Van Daan is caught stealing half a loaf of bread, the other people are extremely angry yet,

surprisingly, it is Mrs Frank who is the hardest on him.
Why do you think this is?

9 'We don't need the Nazis to destroy us' says Mr Frank.
Why is everyone arguing so much at this point?

10 Despite all the horror that Hitler and his Nazi party
have brought, and despite the way in which the people
in the Annex treat each other, Anne says, 'In spite of
everything, I still believe that people are really good at
heart.' Do you agree with her? What does the fact that
Anne can still have faith in human nature and hope for
the future, tell you about her character?

2 Explorations

A Character

Anne Frank

1 In Act One, Scene Three Mrs Frank says to Anne, 'I'm
afraid for other people, that you'll walk on them . . . You are
wild, self-willed.'
Do you think the fact that Anne is sometimes 'wild and self-
willed' means that she will 'walk on' people? Or do you
think she shows concern for others?

2 In Act One, Scene Three Mr Van Daan criticizes Anne for
her behaviour and suggests that she should be more lady-like,
'A man likes a girl who'll listen to him once in a while – a
domestic girl, who'll keep her house shining for her husband
– who loves to cook and sew . . .' Anne replies, 'I'd cut my
throat first. I'd open my veins. I'm going to be remarkable.'

Do you think that Anne is 'remarkable'? If so, in what
ways? What aspects of her character do you think have made
her such an important person to so many people?

Other characters

3 Write two entries for a diary which Peter might keep. The first entry might be shortly after his arrival in the annex (dated some time in 1942); the second entry could be after he and Anne begin to like each other (dated early 1944).

4 Write Miep's (or Mr Kraler's) story: tell why you helped the Frank family, what you did, how difficult it was, what your fears were and how the story ended.

5 Choose three of the characters from the play (excluding Anne). Write their 'goodbye' letters to Anne. What would they say? Would they try to put right anything they did not handle well during their time with Anne? How would they express their feelings about what had happened and what they thought (hoped) the future would hold?

B Drama

Captivity

1 When Anne writes in her diary, she knows that she will miss being able to go outside: 'Never to breathe fresh air – never to run and shout and jump.' She writes later about the things that the others would like to do: 'Mrs Van Daan longs to be home with her own things . . . the Bechstein piano her father gave her – the best that money could buy. Peter would like to go to a movie. Mr Dussel wants to get back to his dentist's drill. For myself . . . to ride a bike again – to laugh till my belly aches – to have new clothes from the skin out . . .'

Write a monologue about how you would feel. Prepare your monologue for presentation and present it to your class or group.

Living conditions and relationships

2   For two whole years Anne, the three members of her family, Mr and Mrs Van Daan and Peter, along with Mr Dussell lived in very cramped conditions. Imagine the strain this put on their relationships. Think about the lack of privacy and about how being unable to go out would have affected them all.

For this activity you need to create a character who you will role-play. Give your character a name. How old is he or she? Think about the way your character will move, walk and talk. What is his or her personality like?

In groups, role-play a situation in which several people have to live together in a small space for some time, without much food. Remember to stay in the role of your character. How does she or he react to the other people?

Nuclear bunker debate

3   For this activity you need to create a character who you will role-play. Give your character a name. How old is she or he? Has she or he any brothers or sisters, sons or daughters? If your character is older, what sort of job does she or he do? If younger what subjects is she or he good at in school? What is your character's personality like? You must think of at least one positive and one negative aspect to your personality.

Nuclear war has begun and you need to get into a shelter to stay alive. There are fewer places in the shelter than there are people. You have one minute to tell your group why you should have a precious place in the shelter.

When each character's presentation has been heard you may ask questions of each other and then you must vote as to who should be offered a place in the shelter and who should not.

Afterwards, think about how you made your decision. Did the rest of the group agree? Is it fair that one life should be 'worth' more than another?

C Further Activities

1 Imagine Otto Frank is still alive (living in Switzerland) and write to him explaining what effect the story of his family has had on you.

2 Write a newspaper article (perhaps a front page) which tells of the discovery of the diary and what it reveals.

3 Imagine you are at school in Germany in the 1930s. One of your friends is Jewish. Describe what happens to him or her and how you react. In the end your friend is removed from the school. In your account, describe how you feel when this happens.

4 Read the following poem and discuss the questions that follow:

> First they came for the Jews
> and I did not speak out –
> because I was not a Jew
> Then they came for the communists
> and I did not speak out –
> because I was not a communist
> Then they came for the trade unionists
> and I did not speak out –
> because I was not a trade unionist
> Then they came for me
> and there was no one left to speak for me
> > *(Pastor Niemoeller*
> > *Victim of the Nazis in Germany)*

Do you think it is important for people to speak out against those with racist ideas? Give reasons for your opinion.

Do you think it is important for us to remember what happened to people like Anne Frank? What are the reasons for your answer?

5 Six million people died in Nazi death camps during the Second World War. Yet despite everything we have learned from the terrible events of the war, Nazi parties in Europe are once more in the news. Whereas in the 1930s Hitler blamed Jews for all economic and social problems, today racists in Britain blame black and Asian people. Because of this, organizations and pressure groups have been set up to prevent racists obtaining the same power as Hitler did in Germany.

Find out about the Anti-Racist, Anti-Nazi movement in Britain today.

6 In the last scene Anne says of the persecution they are suffering: 'I believe the world is going through a phase . . . It'll pass, maybe not for hundreds of years, but some day.'

Drawing on your knowledge of what is happening in the world today, do you think that such treatment of people is now in the past?

7 If you have access to a copy of Anne's diary, compare the dramatized version with the original version. You may find it helpful to think about these points:

- What changes have been made?
- Why do you think the dramatists have altered the diary?
- Do you think the play makes as much or more impact than the diary?

Glossary

ack-ack	anti-aircraft gun
Auf machen!	Open up!
black market	illegal buying and selling
carillon	set of bells that can be rung mechanically
chaise-longue	elegant sofa
Churchill	British Prime Minister during the Second World War
Da drinnen!	In there!
Eisenhower	General in the United States army, Commander in Chief, Allied Forces Europe during the Second World War
Fascism	political movement characterized by nationalism and the suppression of the individual by an authoritarian state controlled by a dictator
fatalist	believer in fate or chance.
Final Solution	Policy of exterminating those considered by the Nazis to be racially inferior to 'Aryan' Germanic people
goloshes	over-shoes
Hanukkah (or **Chanuka**)	Jewish Festival of Lights, which lasts for eight days in December
Hitler	architect of Nazism; Chancellor of Germany 1933–45, dictator
Holocaust	murder of six million Jews by the Nazis in concentration camps between 1940–45
inarticulate	unable to express ideas clearly

insufferable/ intolerable	unbearable
latkas	potato pancakes eaten at the Hanukkah festival
L'chaim	a good luck greeting
liefje	sweetie
Maccabees	Jewish freedom fighters
makes a feint	pretends
Menorah (or Menocah)	special candlestick used in Jewish ceremonies
mercurial	changeable
meticulous	careful
mythology	ancient stories
Nazi	member of Hitler's National Socialist German Workers' Party
nonplussed	confused
ostentatiously	obviously
Schnell!	quickly
stenographer	one who uses shorthand
sustenance	nourishment
zeal	enthusiasm

Bibliography

The Holocaust   Martin Gilbert, Weidenfeld and Nicolson

The Diary of Anne Frank   New Windmill Series, Heinemann Educational

The Fixer   Bernard Malamud, Penguin

Long Journey Home   Julius Lester, Puffin

Six Feet of Country   Nadine Gordimer, Penguin

Friedrich   Hans Peter Richter, New Windmill Series, Heinemann Educational

I Am David   Anne Holm, New Windmill Series, Heinemann Educational

The Devil in Vienna   Doris Orgel, New Windmill Series, Heinemann Educational

The Wave   Morton Rhue, New Windmill Series, Heinemann Educational

DON/11